Endorsements

Written from the heart and filled with love, light and hope, this book will transport readers from grief and despair to wonder and reassurance that their deceased children (and others) are still alive and well in another dimension we usually call heaven. As a bereaved father myself, I recommend *Cracking the Grief Code* to you very, very highly.

—**Bill Guggenheim,** author of *Hello From Heaven*

The brilliant "code" Virginia deciphers is nothing less than a major shift in conscious awareness of what *life truly is!* I was amazed how her beautifully woven story helped tremendously in my own particular grief journey, and I believe will help anyone dealing with losses of any kind.

—**Peter Shockey** Documentary Filmmaker; *Life After Life* / author: *Miracles, Angels & Afterlife*

Virginia Hummel has written a magnificent book, the best I have ever read on the subject of recovering from loss of any kind. It makes a very important contribution to both the professional and lay topical literature, so much so that it may one day rank as a superb seminal work. Whether one is suffering from the pain of losing a loved one, the loss of a marriage or job, or experiencing emotional or psychological difficulties of any kind, *Cracking the Grief Code* will be an enormous help and a terrific resource.

—**John Audette MS** President, CEO & Co-Founder, Eternea, Inc. (eternea.org). Former hospice and hospital administrator and primary founder of the International Association of Near-Death Studies, Inc. (IANDS.org)

I have read so many books on grief since the loss of my thirty-year old son in 2011 and *Cracking the Grief Code* should be a must read for those who are on the path to healing their own grief. Whether you are a newly bereaved, still struggling with old unprocessed grief, or know someone going through this journey, this book will help you reclaim a richer and more fulfilled life.

—**Sandy Arsenault Panek** Reiki Master/Teacher, Massage Therapist

Virginia Hummel has clearly demonstrated her personal and professional expertise in the area of healing grief and the impact that spiritual events can have on our lives. As a hospice nurse case worker, I found *Cracking the Grief Code* to be the ultimate spiritual guide for the dying patient, caregivers, healthcare professionals and anyone who is grieving from loss of a relationship or loved one.

—**Erica McKenzie, BSN, RN** Inspirational Speaker, Advocate, and author of *Dying To Fit In*

Belief is the first key to awakening to the existence of the greater reality and to the continued existence of those who have passed. In *Cracking the Grief Code*, Virginia Hummel provides a wealth of evidence that allows readers to move beyond belief to trust. Bravo for a book that speaks to the heart and mind and helps us to unite with our loved ones across the veil.

—**Suzanne Giesemann,** author of *Messages of Hope* and *Wolf's Message*

CRACKING THE GRIEF CODE

*The Healing Power of the Orb Phenomenon,
After-Death Communication, Near-Death Experiences,
Pre-Birth Contracts, Past Lives and Reincarnation*

Virginia M. Hummel

Copyright © 2017 by Virginia M. Hummel

Certain names and identifying characteristics of people have been changed.

All rights exclusively reserved. No part of this book may be reproduced or translated into any language or utilized in any form or by any means, electronic or mechanical, including photocopying, recording or by any information storage and retrieval system, without permission in writing from the publisher. Reviewers may quote brief passages.

Hummel, Virginia M.– Cracking the Grief Code: The Healing Power of the Orb Phenomenon, After-Death Communication, Near-Death Experiences, Pre-Birth Contracts, Past Lives and Reincarnation

Library of Congress No. 2014922108

ISBN 978-0-9834787-6-8 (Trade Paperback.)
ISBN 978-0-9834787-9-9 (eBook)

Cover: Sherwin Soy
Interior Design: Virginia M. Hummel
Author Photo: Mark Davidson Photography

Due to a lack of quality control for the print on demand (POD) process, sometimes photos in this book may appear distorted. Please visit OrbWhisperer.com to view the colored photos online.

To my granddaughter, Brooklyn
You make my heart sing!

Contents

CONTENTS	XI
AUTHOR'S NOTE	XV
CHAPTER ONE	1
CHAPTER TWO	9
After-Death Communication	9
Code Words	20
CHAPTER THREE	23
Signs and Hints	23
CHAPTER FOUR	39
Pre-Birth Contracts	39
CHAPTER FIVE	51
The Light Being	51
CHAPTER SIX	63
Embrace the Gift	63
CHAPTER SEVEN	77
DMT: The Spirit Molecule (N, N-Dimethyltryptamine)	77
CHAPTER EIGHT	85
Survival of Consciousness	85
Good Vibrations	91
CHAPTER NINE	95
Near-Death Experience and Orbs	95
Corroborating an Orb Experience	100
CHAPTER TEN	107
The Urge to Know	107
Life as an Eternal Being	111
Our Authentic Self	118
CHAPTER ELEVEN	123

Reframing Your Grief Experience	123
The Lesson and the Gift	127
CHAPTER TWELVE	**133**
Permission to Heal	133
Ten Things to Shift Your Thoughts:	138
CHAPTER THIRTEEN	**139**
Think + Feel = Shift	139
Everything is a Miracle	144
CHAPTER FOURTEEN	**153**
Perception	153
How to Raise Your Vibration	155
Outside Influences	157
CHAPTER FIFTEEN	**161**
Manifesting Reality	161
Ripple Effect	165
Thoughts in Action	167
CHAPTER SIXTEEN	**175**
Past Lives	175
CHAPTER SEVENTEEN	**183**
Reincarnation	183
CONCLUSION	**200**
ACKNOWLEDGEMENTS	**203**
READING LIST	**205**
BIBLIOGRAPHY	**206**
ENDNOTES	**210**
ABOUT THE AUTHOR	**217**

© Paul Mahal. Virginia Hummel with an orb.

"When we lift our perceived limitations off the traditional grief experience, we lift our perceived limitations off our ability to heal."

~ Virginia Hummel

AUTHOR'S NOTE

Sometimes we're given the opportunity to recognize the truth behind a message with absolute clarity. In that moment, we can choose to stand with that truth and reconnect with our divine self, or simply go on with our lives as before.

For me, however, it felt as if there was no choice. When that moment arrived, I was compelled to act from deep within. On February 4, 2006, I received my opportunity or "message of truth" with a telephone call that my beautiful son Christopher, age twenty-five, had been killed in an accident. From the depths of my heartbreak, I heard a call to service. It was a defining moment that has brought me here to you.

This book has found its way into your hands through the miracle and grace of Spirit. It is a work of love from me to you with the deepest hope that it may help to lift the sadness from your heart and bring you comfort by showing you the magnificent eternal nature of our souls.

The information, stories, and photos may challenge you to step beyond your perception of the traditional grief experience and your ability to heal after the loss of a loved one. You may drop the book and exclaim, "No way. That's not possible!" or you may jump for joy and say, "That happened to me too!" Either way, it could be a catalyst for transformation on a deep level. I believe that if you are reading this book there is a part of you ready for the next step in your spiritual evolution.

This is a book about healing grief through the power of thought, vibration and Spiritually Transformative Experiences (STEs). I do not dwell on the agony of loss, but strive to demonstrate that along with loss comes a miraculous connection to Spirit that began long before

CRACKING THE GRIEF CODE

we were born and continues on long after we "die." Woven throughout this book are excerpts from my previously written book, "Miracle Messenger." I have chosen to include them to expand upon these experiences with input from others who have had the same or similar experiences and to show that these kinds of occurrences are more common than not.

The grief journey is different for everyone. We have basic road maps, but no definitive way to grieve. Some of us can and do heal. For others, it can take a lifetime to find a place of acceptance for their loss. It is important to honor our feelings of loss in whatever form they manifest. We miss the physical presence of our family member or friend and the void left by their death can seem overwhelming.

It is also important not to set limits on our grief journey or our ability to heal. We can begin the healing process immediately. Yes, it is a process to find our balance, but when we lift our perceived limitations off the traditional grief experience, we can also lift our perceived limitations off our ability to heal. We realize anything is possible, even healing our grief.

Healed grief does not mean we forget our loved one or no longer experience moments of sadness. Healed grief means being able to talk about and honor our loved one in a proactive, positive way, and go on to participate in a life that includes joy and laughter. For many, it also means that we can continue to have a relationship with our loved one through the miracle of Spirit.

For me, it started with the appearance of a brilliant ball of light or orb, twenty months after the death of my son. From there, it led to people, places, research and experiences that revealed the workings of a divine plan and clues to our eternal nature hidden in plain sight. My grief

AUTHOR'S NOTE

journey ultimately led me to a perception of death that has been a metamorphosis, rebirth and awakening to Spirit.

As I opened myself to the possibilities of something more, I reached outside the limited boundaries of science, religion and familial teachings. Through my time of bereavement and healing, this Spiritual connection has provided a sense of comfort and peace unlike any other.

I have worked hard to release the sadness and despair of my son's death, and with the wonderful connection and support from Spirit, I have embraced life with joy and happiness. Now I can speak of Christopher with love, fond smiles and laughter. That truth, however, stands side by side with this truth: On occasion, I will tear up just because I miss my son's physical presence, his hugs and his smile.

My son's death did not define me; it inspired me to search for answers, be of service and ultimately discover the lessons and the gifts in one of life's most challenging experiences. But before I share the stories from those who have used the power of thought and Spiritually Transformative Experiences (STEs) to heal their grief, I feel it is important to offer a brief picture of where I started on this journey of healing so that you may understand what can be possible after the death of a child or loved one.

What would it feel like to transform your grief?

CHAPTER ONE

"I can do all things through Him who strengthens me."
~ Philippians 4:13

Cracking the Grief Code

When I was eight years old, I stood alone in my parents' driveway and stared at a brilliant blue sky that was cloudless and perfect. I can remember that moment as if it were yesterday—the heat of the asphalt beneath my sneakers, the smell of freshly mowed grass, and the colorful array of mid-summer blooms in my mother's garden.

Yet, in spite of the beauty of nature surrounding me, sadness tugged at my heart. I felt abandoned, lost, set adrift to find my way alone as if someone had played a cruel joke on me. I had the knowledge or intuitive *knowing* that I'd been given a set of instructions, ones that I had agreed to undertake, but, as I stared at my empty hands, I felt like I'd failed before I began.

Vaguely, I recalled a list of things I needed to do, with specific reasons for doing them—but I had no idea what they were. Had I taken notes? If so, where were they? In fact, I didn't know who I really was or how I came to be in this body.

I pinched my arm. I was here all right. My flesh was warm and firm, but my mind cried out with confusion. *How did I get to be me and not someone else?*

Knowing I came from "somewhere else" meant I must be "returning again," but I had the distinct feeling I was on the outside looking in. Surely, there must have been a mistake. As I stared at my dog lying comfortably beneath the shade of an apple tree, I thought to myself, "Why didn't I *come back* as my dog, or as my brother…or even as my mother?"

The Knowing

On the day my son Christopher was born, I held him in my arms and love poured from my heart. I was swept up in the miracle of that precious moment. I had always thought that if you didn't believe there was a God, you would surely change your mind the moment you held your newborn in your arms. Love for Chris bloomed instantly.

Yet in the midst of my joy as I held my baby for the first time, I also experienced a *knowing* that shook me to my core.

I knew my son would die before I did.

At the birth of Chris's three siblings, I'd never had this same sense of *knowing*. For twenty-five years, I prayed for Chris's safety and I prayed the prophetic voice was wrong. Then one bright Saturday morning in February 2006, my brother Peter called.

"The police just left my house. Chris was killed last night in a motorcycle accident," he blurted out.

"What?" I gasped. My mind reeled. "Are you—*sure?*"

"Yes," Peter said. "I'm sure."

A lifetime of memories with my son flashed before me. I'd warned Chris of the dangers of riding a motorcycle. Now living away from home and on his own, he hadn't told me that he'd bought one.

Stunned, I sank against my desk. As if I'd been holding my breath for twenty-five years, in one gigantic exhalation I released all my pent-up anxiety and fear. Oh, God…it was finally over and my beautiful son was gone.

As waves of excruciating pain crashed over me, from somewhere deep within, I realized I was feeling something else. Along with the unfathomable ache of loss was also a sense of relief. I knew without a doubt that my son was safe.

He was Home.

My young daughter Olivia burst into tears at the news. As I numbly gathered her in my arms to hold and comfort, I knew I would never hold or see my son again. He was gone—forever.

This was the first time in my life someone I deeply loved died. I wanted to scream at the top of my lungs. I wanted to grab him and shake the life back into his still body. I wanted to fall to my knees and beg God to trade my life for his—and I wanted God to take me too. How could He leave me here to feel the dark hole of my son's absence? How could I stay here without him?

The fierce ache of knowing it was too late gripped every part of my being. More than anything I wanted a second chance to do everything right. Marching before me were all the mistakes I'd made as a young mother. How could I have let precious moments with my child pass me by, simply because I was caught up in daily life with its constant demands?

Recently, we were to meet a few weeks earlier in Los Angeles for lunch, but Chris called and asked if he could go golfing with his friends instead. At the time, I was tired and relented, assuming I would see him during Easter, a month or so away.

Why hadn't I insisted we meet? It would have been one last hug goodbye and the chance to tell him again, how much I loved him.

Yet, here was the irony: my heart ached with loss and separation, *yet my soul remained oddly calm and at peace.* How was that possible when my child was dead?

A furious battle raged within, between the spiritual revelations I had just experienced...*my son was safe...He was Home...*and the horror of knowing *my child was gone.*

I wanted to collapse in a heap and wail until every bit of pain was obliterated, but instead, I was filled with the most incredible feelings of strength and love. *In that moment, I knew that I must cling to every experience in my life that had told me there is neither death nor separation from our loved ones who have left this world.* I also knew if I let go of that thought, I would never survive this loss.

When we arrived at the Ventura County Coroner's office on the weekend of my son's accident, my two daughters, two of my four brothers, and my niece waited while I went in to say goodbye. I stood at the end of the hallway and braced myself. Forcing one weighted foot in front of the other, I reluctantly moved toward the room where Chris lay. If only I could turn and run in the opposite direction.

Honestly, I wanted someone else to go first, to do this for me. I wanted to hide behind my dad's leg and cling to his trousers like I did as a child when I was scared. I wanted someone to hold me and tell me everything would be all right.

But there was no one to comfort me except myself. Chris's father and I had divorced when he was six months old. I steeled myself for what I was about to see and slowly pushed open the door to the small viewing room.

Through the glass windows across the room, I caught a glimpse of my son's body. I gasped as if I'd been punched in the chest. As I clutched my heart against the impact of the blow, I realized the truth had not yet had a chance to solidify. *Chris's death was not yet real.* I clamped my hand over my mouth to keep from screaming at the horror of it all.

A single errant tear slid down my cheek as I willed myself not to break down. Repelled by the glass that separated us, I was simultaneously drawn toward it. I didn't want this to be true, but I could clearly see that it was. My beautiful son lay on a gurney covered in pristine white sheets tucked up to his chin. They had already performed the autopsy.

Having watched numerous medical shows on television, I knew what lay beneath those sheets, yet I took in every inch of the scene before me. Mentally, I touched Chris with my hands and ran my fingers through his sandy brown hair. I stroked his brow, kissed his cheek and held him as if he were an infant. How did we end up here like this, and why? What was the purpose of this seemingly senseless loss of life?

Envisioning the accident and my son's last moments, I wondered did he cry out for me? Was he afraid? Did he know he was going to die? How could I have not known that he needed me? I was his mother. I had held him when he entered this world, if only I could have held him when he left.

A Second Awakening

As I stood there feeling sorry for myself, regretting the decisions that may have landed both of us in this position, I became aware of something that was more than just me. This "something" momentarily sucked me from my shock.

A shift somewhere within was causing me to feel separate, yet part of everything around me. Then I began to vibrate. As crazy as it seems, I felt as if I were swimming in champagne. I became acutely aware of the room, the molecules in the air and the walls, the sound or lack of it, and the infinitesimal flicker of the fluorescent lighting. It was surreal. I didn't know what was happening. *What I did know was that my son was not in that body lying before me...and he was not dead.*

The experience was profoundly life altering on many levels: first, as a mother who would never again physically hold her child; second, as a grandmother who grieved for the little boy he left behind; and third and most important, as a non-physical Higher or Inner Self that was confirming without a doubt that there are two distinct and separate parts to a human being: the physical and spiritual.

Standing in the small viewing room, I knew I was seeing Chris's shell: a temporary home for an eternal being. I felt physically frozen, yet everywhere at once. This duality was exactly what I had experienced at the age of eight, standing in the middle of my driveway, feeling separate from my body and wondering why I hadn't returned to this lifetime as my dog, my brother, or even my mother. At the age of eight, I knew I had existed somewhere else outside of my physical body and now I was receiving confirmation that Chris had returned to that non-physical existence and that same "somewhere else."

Brad Steiger, author of *One with the Light: Authentic Near-Death Experiences that Changed Lives and Revealed the Beyond*, tells of ten-year-old Randy Gehling's near-death experience (NDE) in 1988 after being struck by a car.[1] After his guardian angel pulled him through the tunnel and into the light, Randy says, "...I kind of felt as if my body exploded—in a nice way—and became a million different atoms—and each single atom could think its own thoughts and have its own feelings. All at once, I seemed to feel like I was a boy, a girl, a dog, a cat, a fish. Then I felt like I was an old man, an old woman—and then a little tiny baby."[2]

Was Randy Gehling experiencing his lives as an eternal soul? At eight years old, standing on my driveway, did I have a similar experience in which I recognized my non-physical form and reconnected to that eternal part of me that delivered memories of other lifetimes, other reincarnations? Now as I stood in the viewing room staring at my son, was I experiencing that same feeling or *knowing* of being an eternal soul?

It would take four decades of challenging life experiences and the death of my beloved child before I was brought to this moment of illumination that revealed the larger picture of who we were, linking past to present. Here were the clues to our eternal nature, hidden in plain sight.

As a child, I didn't realize the importance of my ability to grasp the true essence of ourselves and that we are "Spirit" or spiritual energy having a human experience. I had not been taught anything about life after death other than the belief that we "go to Heaven" after we die. That one moment on the driveway when I wondered why I had returned in *this* body was the first step in my process of awakening or "remembering," as I like to refer to it now. It was a big thought for a little girl, yet it came so naturally. It was my first opportunity to discover my role as an eternal being.

Now, I realized that my experience in the viewing room and that earlier scene on the driveway as an eight-year-old were connected. Somehow, I instinctively knew with absolute clarity that Chris's death was a catalyst for me to discover my mission in life, the one I had forgotten as a child. This was a chance to experience what I had already known since childhood.

We don't die.

At that moment, my spiritual self felt such a trust and connection with God and the Universe. After all, I thought, this wasn't about me; it was about Chris and his time to cross. Only later did I come to understand that it really *was* about me and my identity as an eternal being. It was about listening to my inner guidance, my higher self and God. It no longer mattered what others thought, believed or practiced.

As I stared through the glass at my little boy, my spiritual self realized that neither Chris nor I were victims, but very important pieces in the puzzle called Life. Given this chance, I was compelled to take it.

My spiritual self knew I had to step beyond my pain and loss and view my grief from a larger perspective. Both life and death had meaning and purpose. I was being given an opportunity for greater awareness. It was part of the "mission" that I had forgotten as a child.

My intuition told me I would become a catalyst to help shift the perception of the traditional grief experience. It began by becoming a role model for my family and friends. They would take their cues from me and it was up to me to show them a new way to perceive this event. *No*, I told myself, *I wouldn't let them down.*

Something inside me knew I had chosen this as part of my earthly experience, *my mission*. It was my lesson and I needed to remember why. I leaned against the window that separated me from my son. It was like the invisible veil that separated us from Spirit, I thought as I stared at my little boy one last time. I prayed to God for help and guidance in this challenging journey ahead. It would be the test of a lifetime and I couldn't do it alone.

"God, please let me know that Chris is okay." I took a deep breath and exhaled slowly to steady myself. A wave of pain washed over me, breaking my lofty thoughts. I cried out, "Oh God, Christopher, I'm so sorry…" and then dropped my head in my hands and cried.

A few minutes later, I quietly I left the room and headed down the hallway toward my family waiting in the lobby. I could barely look at them for fear they would see the pain that almost buckled my knees.

My daughter Kristin asked to see her brother alone. As she started down the hallway, I steeled myself once again, my heart breaking yet mentally trying to bolster her strength to survive the next few minutes. My son and daughter had been so close. We heard the door open. Her scream resounded throughout the hallway and lobby, piercing my heart for the second time that day. It was the same scream of shock and loss that I had wanted to release, but knew for the sake of my family that I could not.

Reaching deep inside for every bit of strength and courage I could muster, I drew on all my years of athletic competition to find that place of ultimate focus and concentration, that inner place of unwavering confidence and faith in my ability to prevail over mind and body. In that place that I'd used for show jumping, gymnastics, and springboard diving, I knew that fear was my greatest enemy and faith my greatest ally.

Whenever my heart and the world screamed separation and loss, I vowed to use those experiences of self-mastery to find the courage and strength to follow my inner *knowing* and reconnect with God and Spirit. It would be extremely challenging to navigate this loss as a parent in grief. However, I knew the only way through the days ahead was to prove what my spiritual self already knew; that life is truly eternal.

CHAPTER TWO

"Everything you were looking for
was right there with you all along."
~ The Wizard of Oz

After-Death Communication

Like a drowning person, I struggled to fight my way through seemingly insurmountable waves of pain and heartbreak. Many times I could barely think or function. However, I was a single mom and I still had my youngest daughter to raise. She still needed to be cared for and driven to school.

My car became my place of refuge. I cried while I drove. I sobbed while I drove. I screamed while I drove. It didn't matter where, but I usually waited until Olivia was at school. I was fine one minute then thoughts of Chris would fill my head. I'd reach for the radio and *You're Beautiful* by James Blunt would start to play. Tears would fall as the haunting sounds of his guitar and lyrics spoke of love and separation, an angel and his brilliant life. Each time I could feel Chris's energy fill the car and I knew he was sitting next to me.

Instinctively, I would lay my arm across the armrest, palm face up and I knew he was holding my hand. I was filled with deep love and pain at the same time. I cried enough tears to fill that car. It was the one place I could let my heart break.

In the midst of my pain and deep sorrow, I also forced myself to remain open and alert to any type of contact with Christopher. I had taught him about life after death. I knew if we really did live on after we had shed our physical body, then Chris would let me know.

He did. Contact started immediately and I was thrilled with each experience. The lights would blink unexpectedly or unusual coincidences would happen and immediately thoughts of Chris would fill my mind. Many times, I would even feel his presence in the room and my skin would explode with goose bumps. To me it was unmistakable, but when I would try to explain what I was experiencing, the magic of the experience was somehow lost in translation.

One of the many profound events happened a few weeks after my son's accident. I was sitting at my desk in front of the computer paying bills. My screensaver flashed random family pictures at five-second intervals from a gallery of thousands. I wasn't really paying attention to the somewhat disjointed montage and the memories they stirred until a picture of Chris appeared the screen. I glanced at the picture and went back to paying my bills. A few moments later, I glanced at the computer again. The picture of Chris was still there. It had frozen on the screen.

My intuition shouted "Pay Attention!" Clearly, something was happening. I sat back in my chair and stared at the screen. Chris stared back at me. He was bare-chested and looking slightly downward with a dimple and a knowing smile. He seemed to be experiencing a secret joy and waiting for me to "get it."

Suddenly the energy in the room shifted. The air seemed charged with a tingly electrical current and raised goose bumps on my skin. The lighting became somehow different, almost surreal. As if he had walked into the room, I could feel his presence surrounding me.

"Chris, you're here," I whispered.

Instantly, I was wrapped in warmth as if a blanket had been placed around my shoulders. Then I felt heat, as if someone had poured thick warm syrup through a hole in the top of my head. The warmth spiraled slowly downward until it filled my entire being, bathing me in complete love, peace, and comfort. It was an incredible feeling.

My heart swelled with love and gratitude for this beautiful experience I had been given and I sat there long after the warmth had disappeared. I knew Chris had wrapped his arms around me and kissed the top of my head. His presence momentarily released me from my grief. Filling me with joy, it validated my inner *knowing* that he was still alive and merely in another form.

It was exciting to share another new contact experience with my friends and family, even if they did not believe in life after death. Afterward, I realized it was a mistake. This type of non-physical experience was so foreign to them; they thought my grief had caused me to take leave of my senses. Rather than shifting their perception of death, they murmured sympathetically, "Oh, you poor baby. You are so deep in grief, you're imagining things. Chris isn't still here. He's gone. Let go and accept it."

It was extremely difficult to listen to what my intuition was telling me—that Christopher was okay—when everyone around me was in such mourning over their loss. I didn't want people's sympathy; I wanted their acknowledgement that what I was experiencing was real. I wanted validation from others that he was still with us. I wanted someone to stand with me, to tell me that my son was still okay, that he was safe and he was home. In order to survive this loss, I needed their support.

Instead of cheerleaders, however, I found myself surrounded by people gripped with a feeling of deep irremediable sadness. Like a powerful tide, it tried to suck me down and under. Would I please join the rest of my family in their grief?

Everyone was so broken by this loss; I realized I was on my own to experience it from a different perspective. Yet even though I knew this task was part of my mission, I was only human. It was all I could do to lift myself out of my own misery and up toward the Light, let alone coax anyone else to see it from my perspective.

When others didn't acknowledge my experiences as real, I was overcome by feelings of doubt and separation. This programming had been planted deep inside when I was a child. It told me I shouldn't listen to my inner guidance, God and my heart, because it wasn't the truth; that when we leave our physical bodies, there really is nothing more.

Seed of Doubt

These childhood doubts and fears sparked a memory, a link to the past that provided a clue to uncovering the time when these seeds of doubt were first planted. I remembered a family trip to Yosemite when I was six. My parents, my three brothers and I hiked along a gravel road beneath towering pine trees near Half Dome, the park's most familiar landmark. Off to one side of the road was a beautiful meadow with tall grass that rippled with the breeze. A short distance away from the road I spotted a doe and her fawn grazing.

My heart leapt with joy as I delighted in the discovery of two of God's beautiful creatures. I was overcome with a desire to hug the baby and share my love for her. I wanted to feel her soft, warm fur and hold her close. Following my heart and trusting my inner guidance, I stretched out my hand and walked toward the two, fully confident they would respond to my love.

Both the mama and baby stopped grazing and raised their heads to watch me as I approached. They were so beautiful and I was filled with such joy, this meeting seemed like the most natural thing for me to do. Fearless, I could feel only love. Then, as if she could feel my love for her, the baby stepped away from her mother and began to wobble toward me on her four spindly legs.

As I stretched out my fingertips, I closed the distance between us. It was as if we knew each other's hearts. We were one; there was no separation between us.

Just as I was about to touch the fawn, my mother yelled out to me, "Don't touch it! Come back here!"

The fawn bolted and the spell was broken. The magic was gone. As if I'd been slapped, my heart closed in fear. Unconsciously I began to question the wisdom of my inner guidance and doubt our spiritual connection to all things.

Even though I knew she was only concerned for my safety, I was angry with my mother. As I grew to adulthood, I observed that her thoughts and reactions were always rooted in fear. Had that fear also closed the connection to God and her inner guidance?

The answer to my question arrived a few weeks after Chris's death when I had my first vivid dream in which my son was present. In my dream, I was at my mom's house in Reno where I had grown up. Chris said it would always be his home. All my living relatives were arriving to express their condolences. As I passed from room to room, a dark cloak of grief hung in the air. Deeply sad people conversed in reverent whispers. I couldn't understand why everyone was so sad when I was excited and happy for my son because I knew the wonders of the other side.

Acutely aware that Chris had only dropped his body and was in spirit form, I realized that no one seemed to understand. I knew he was now vibrant and alive. I tried to tell them and kept thinking, *why don't they get it?*

Maybe if I had proof…

So I stepped outside on the patio and walked around to the back of the house until I reached the driveway near our fenced orchard. My mom and oldest brother Bill were standing there talking softly. I glanced up at the sky. It was so blue, so beautiful, scattered with only a few large clouds. As I gazed at its brilliant blue color and at the fluffy white clouds, my heart filled with love and joy.

In one of the voluminous clouds, I noticed an opening. Streaming through this opening was a glittering gold ticker tape displaying the names of all our relatives who had crossed over. I remembered seeing some of those names once or twice on our genealogy chart but would not have been able to recall them. I could hear their voices cheering and chattering excitedly.

"Chris is here! He's okay." They said. "He's arrived safely." Their excitement about Chris's arrival filled me with happiness and comforted my heart. It confirmed my *knowing* that he was safe and there really was something more beyond this earthly existence than we're led to believe.

Grabbing my brother, I pointed to the sky. "Look! Can you see them? It's amazing. See? I told you!"

Squinting and shading his eyes, Bill looked up, and then shook his head. "Where? I don't see anything."

Then I turned to my mother. "Mom, look! Chris is okay! He's with all of them. Can't you see? Can't you hear them?"

My mother didn't even try to look up. Letting out a deep sigh, she bowed her head. Her shoulders curled inward around her heart. "No, I can't," she said.

Waves of sadness and despair washed over me. I felt my mother's fear and separation. She seemed so lost and alone. She had always said she wouldn't know what to do if she lost my brother Bill or my son Chris. I felt so sad for both my mother and my brother. I looked up again and actually waved at the entire group of relatives who had already crossed over.

Despite my mother's sadness, my own heart was full of love and joy. I could see beyond the veil. My son was home and he was safe.

The next morning I called my mom and related my dream of the night before. "Mom, in the dream, I got the distinct impression that you don't believe in life after death. You believe that once they put your body in the ground, it's the end. You also believe that when your father, mother and brother died they had abandoned you and left you here, alone."

She started to cry. "Yes, that's exactly what I believe."

Stunned by her confession, I had never thought to question my mother's beliefs about death, but I had discovered in my dream exactly how she felt. Now she was confirming the information I had received.

After Death Communication (ADC)

Later, I learned these dreams are called after-death communications or ADCs. In 1995, Bill and Judy Guggenheim co-authored a book called *Hello From Heaven! A New Field of Research: After-Death Communication Confirms That Life and Love Are Eternal*, which states:

> After-Death Communication (ADC) is a spiritual experience, which occurs when you are contacted directly and spontaneously by a deceased family member or friend, without the use of psychics, mediums, rituals, or devices of any kind[3]…Sleep-state ADCs feel like actual face-to-face visits with deceased loved ones. They are much more orderly, colorful, vivid, and memorable than most dreams.[4]

There have been a dozen or so "sleep-state" or dream ADCs since my son crossed, five of which included Christopher. They always left me feeling that he was alive and well on the other side. In the nine years following the death of my son, I had the opportunity to connect with Spirit on a regular basis through many different types of ADCs.

After-death contact can include sightings, smells like fragrances or cigars, dreams, visions or songs. We may hear a voice; feel a presence or even receive a phone call or voice message from our loved one. Spirit can use electronic equipment to communicate too. We might see the lights flicker or have something unusual happen with the radio, iPod, iPad, TV or computer.

Loved ones on the other side have even sent text messages. They can also leave handwritten notes. Spirit sometimes uses animals as a comforting sign from our loved ones, along with the appearance of feathers, flowers, coins, butterflies, birds, and dragonflies among other things. You may discover a sign unique to you and your loved one.

Our intuition or sixth sense alerts us to these signs through a thought or feeling and it is important that we pay attention. The challenge with being deep in grief is that it's difficult to notice Spirit and we can miss the opportunities our loved ones make trying to connect with us.

Grief and Spirit are at opposite ends of the spectrum. Grief is a dense, low vibrational state whereas Spirit is a light, fast vibrational state. When we only focus on our pain and loss, our ability to recognize the signs from the afterlife is hindered. Similar to our cell phone being out of range and losing its signal, we must make a conscious effort to reconnect. This is especially important in the early stages of our grief when our loved ones reach out with a comforting message or sign.

Austyn

Austyn Wells is a Spiritual Medium. I had a brilliant reading with her during the filming of my grief documentary. Not only did my son come through in the reading, she validated what I had discovered on my own journey during grief while trying to connect with spirit. Austyn says:

> A part of our body goes into fight or flight when we are newly in grief. One of the symptoms or ways our body works through fight or flight is by narrowing our visual ability to *see*. This is why a person in grief can't see the signs and symbols of Spirit around them.
>
> Grief is so dense that we can't feel anything other than our grief, so we must make a concerted effort to pay attention and connect. There are so many parents in grief that can't find their way without their child but what they need to know is that the child can't wait until they know that they are there.

As a mother, I developed "mommy radar" when my children were born. Somehow my child and I were connected and I knew when they needed me. It was an unspoken telepathic connection and it is common for parents, especially mothers, to have this connection. Now, as a mother whose child has died, I find my new role is developing "mommy spiritual radar" in order to connect with my son who has crossed over. This spiritual radar and our ability to connect is an important component of our grief healing journey.

After-death communication can come through mediums, psychics, friends or relatives but my favorite is when I personally experience it. With each contact I received knowledge, comfort, or help from Spirit. I was uplifted during a time of deep grief. Through my ADC experiences, I have also discovered that we can ask for this contact or "sign" from our loved one and many times get immediate results. It no longer appears to be limited to just a spontaneous event. I remember one such experience that happened a few years ago.

During a large Thanksgiving reunion with eighty relatives and extra household help, I had purposely set my wallet aside for safe keeping. The night before I had planned to fly home I could not remember where I had hidden it. I needed my ID to board the plane the following day and tore the house apart looking for it to no avail. My suitcase was in my mother's room and I returned there, once again, to recheck the area for my wallet.

Desperate and frustrated, I called out to my son and demanded action. "Christopher Arrington, you help me find my wallet right now!" Crossing my arms, I waited impatiently for it to magically appear in front of me. When it didn't, I spun on my heels, exasperated, and headed out of her bedroom.

Just as I crossed the threshold from her room to the hallway, an unseen force pulled me up short. It felt as if two hands had grasped my shoulders. Snapped to attention, I stood uncharacteristically erect before I was marched down the hall and stopped in front of my old bedroom. It felt as if I were a puppet.

Then I executed a military precision ninety degree turn to my left, took three steps forward, halted, executed another ninety degree turn and had my head shoved toward a wire basket hanging on the wall. Inside was my wallet exactly where I had hidden it five days before. I was dumfounded and ashamed at the same time for throwing a little tantrum and demanding his help. I immediately apologized to Chris for my behavior, thanked him profusely, and ran to share my experience with my two daughters.

Through my after-death communications with Spirit and my son, I realized that I could give my mother and the rest of my family hope that there was something more than just this life. I decided to relay all my experiences with Chris and Spirit and continue to talk openly about life after death, no matter how crazy people might think I was or how difficult it would be to stifle my seed of doubt and listen to my intuition and to God.

Shortly after Chris's accident, I received a package of his personal effects from the coroner's office. Inside were his wallet, cell phone, loose change, and his watch. My heart ached as I touched each item. Somehow, I hoped to feel my son and experience a last connection to his physical form. I would have given anything to be able to hug him goodbye.

When I used his cell phone, it made me feel like I still had a connection to him. I would call his phone number to hear his voice message, then scroll through the contacts and notify his friends. I also fielded phone calls. Three times, in two days, his phone rang and I answered to silence on the other end. Yet I always felt that someone was listening. Someone was there. I knew in my heart that it was Chris trying to communicate with me. When I redialed the number shown on the phone, a voice recording said, "This number is no longer in service."

Hmmm...I smiled. At least he was trying.

Every time I had a contact experience with Chris, it lifted me from grief to a place of joy. When I asked family and friends if they had experienced anything, I discovered that some of them were also having contact with him. Chris's lifelong friend, Mandi Paterson, received multiple phone calls the weekend of my son's death from an all zero number (000) 000-0000. Each time she answered, she could faintly hear a voice at the other end.

Mandi was unaware that Chris had died the weekend of the calls or that those who have crossed over can use electricity and electronic devices to contact us. Since there were so many of those "zero number" calls that weekend, she imagined someone might be stalking her. She contacted her cell phone provider, who told her there was no record of the calls and there was no number with all zeros. We both concluded that Chris had attempted to contact her. I was relieved and thrilled that someone else had experienced contact with Chris. *I wasn't crazy.*

When I mentioned the all zero number (000) 000-0000 and contact with my son, some people were quick to point out that the all zero number was nothing more than a telemarketer number. Yet Melinda Shelton and Cathy Johnson VanHorn also experienced a meaningful connection with their loved ones through an all zero number (000) 000-0000.

Melinda

Melinda Shelton had contact with her deceased mother through the telephone too in the form of a written message. She says:

> Right after my mom passed away, I had really bad insomnia. I was awake one night thinking about all of the shouldas, couldas, wouldas and the phone rang. It wasn't the normal 'Ring Ring', but one continual ringing. I looked at the caller ID (it shown on the TV screen via our cable provider), and it was all zeros (000) 000-0000 and in place of the name it read, *rest sis*. It stopped ringing once I had read it. My mom and family called me 'Sis' since I was born. After I caught my breath and stopped shaking, I lay down and finally slept.

I one thousand percent believe that it was my mother calling me. There is absolutely no other explanation for the ringing, the timing, and that particular message in place of the caller's name. She knew how badly I needed to rest and let me know it was okay.

Cathy

Cathy Johnson VanHorn's brother had been quite ill until contact from the other side through the telephone. She says:

> During a time of fervent family prayers for my very ill brother, I had a phone call. It was just one ring. The caller ID showed (000) 000-0404. I tried to call it back and discovered it was not a working number. The numbers 0404 had been the last four digits of our deceased parent's phone number for the last forty-five years of their lives. We were so overjoyed with this sign from our parents and our brother soon recovered.

My experience has shown me that after-death communication can appear in unexpected and miraculous ways and at just the right moment. Many times, we may be too deep in grief to notice signs from Spirit so they enlist others to help relay a message from our loved one. These messages can offer comfort or information to aid in our healing. A reputable psychic or medium can also do this.

Code Words

The latest way to validate that our loved one lives on is with a code word. We create code words between two or more people while alive. Whoever crosses over first will use that particular word to communicate that they are still "alive" on the other side. The code word may come through a gifted friend, acquaintance, psychic or medium. Spirit has also been known to use the TV, text messages and a host of other ADC's so be aware that your validation can come through in any form.

It is important to choose an unusual word as a means to validate the connection with our deceased loved one but we should still be able to visualize the word we choose. That way a psychic, friend or acquaintance, who might not understand what our loved one is trying to say, may be able to interpret a picture of it instead. For example, if my code word was Cincinnati, the name of my cat, the messenger would still be able to describe a cat even if he couldn't get the name totally correct. Or they may offer something along the lines of, "Are you planning a trip to Cincinnati?"

Because it is an unusual word, we know it would be less likely that the messenger guessed and that it was a real connection with our loved one. We may also see or hear the code word several times in a row after our loved one has crossed over.

Code words can be places or things or whatever is most meaningful to you. Creating a code word with loved ones is a proactive way to embrace the idea of life after death and then experience it once your loved one crosses.

Recently, I was visiting my friend Susan Parker whose husband had crossed several years ago. During my visit, Susan mentioned she could feel Cort's presence in the room. I am clairsentient, which means I can feel when spirit moves into the room. I am also able to receive downloads and information for people from the other side. As I was describing the use of the code word, I hesitated, searching my mind for an unusual word when suddenly, "crawdad" flew out of my mouth.

Susan gasped and said that was totally Cort! He used to love to prepared huge crawdad feasts on his boat each summer. It was a highlight for him. She asked why I had chosen that particular word and I said, "I don't know. It just popped into my mind and flew out of my mouth." Crawdad was a beautiful example of how a meaningful word can validate the presence of a loved one. Even though Susan and Cort had never created a code word, that particular word was unusual and had meaning for both of them. It validated Susan's intuition that Cort was still nearby.

AFTER-DEATH COMMUNICATION

While many of us receive signs from our loved ones after they have crossed over, many of us also receive signs when a loved one is preparing to cross over.

CHAPTER THREE

> "The only way to discover the limits of the possible
> is to go beyond them into the impossible."
> ~ Arthur C. Clark

Signs and Hints

Sometimes we are able to look back on an experience with a new perspective. We are able to see things we had not seen before. The death of a loved one is no exception. Something happened with both Mandi Paterson and her mother the weekend my son Christopher died. They each reported an unexplained bright light that appeared in their bedrooms.

The appearance of the bright light faded from focus because something else continued to bother me. How had I known that of the two of us, Christopher would be the first to die? Where did this information come from?

Memories soon surfaced and I realized that on the evening of Chris's accident, hours before his death, I'd had a premonition. I'd gone to bed early and as I lay there, the oddest thought entered my mind. *Here I was in bed relaxing while my son was lying dead in a ditch somewhere.* I don't know what possessed me to have that awful, totally unfounded thought at that particular moment.

A few hours later, they found my son lying in a ditch. I hadn't made the connection until I viewed the coroner's photographs of the accident scene that had been enclosed in the package with his personal items. The timing was uncanny. I was stunned. How did I know this information and where did this knowledge or *knowing* come from? I now realized that I needed to find answers to these questions to make sense of his early death and release the guilt I felt for being unable to prevent it.

In addition to the message I'd received at Chris's birth, I now recalled the time my son came to me as a teenager and quite matter-of-factly told me he knew when and how he was going to die. I was shocked he would mention something like this. I'd never told anyone about the message I'd received at Chris's birth. I begged him to share his information with me but at first, he refused. He said he wanted to protect me. When I persisted, he still refused to part with his information until several years later. At that time, he told me he would die when he was "52."

When I received the phone call from my brother, Peter, on February 4, 2006 telling me that Chris died in a motorcycle accident, my deepest sorrow had come true. It wasn't until several months after Chris's death that I remembered and reflected on what he'd told me when he was a teenager, i.e. that he would die at age 52. *But he died at age 25*, I reminded myself. Then instantly, in my mind's eye the numbers reversed themselves. I knew that he had deliberately misled me to spare me the heartache and worry. This *knowing* was the same kind of *knowing* I had on the day he was born.

How had my son known when he was going to die? Why did I receive a *knowing* at his birth, reminders throughout his life, and a premonition the night of his death? What was the purpose in knowing ahead of time and being forewarned of this loss? I could only reasonably conclude that not only was there something more to this life than what we could see, this had to have been a plan that had preceded Chris's birth and possibly even mine.

Realizing that both my son and I knew of his impending death, I was compelled to look for a larger meaning, to dig deeper into the supposition that we are eternal beings. That was the only explanation that made sense. Could my *knowing* have been a memory from a spiritual contract my son and I made before we incarnated into these bodies?

If so, then why had we chosen to participate in his early death? What were the lessons to be learned? What had his life and early passing taught me? How could I honor my son and our journey if not to remain in a state of grace and be open to his contact as well as the other experiences available to me?

The Preparation

Soon another memory and experience surfaced to help me connect the dots. In December 2005, about six weeks prior to Chris's death, I was introduced to a man who had lost his college-aged daughter in an auto accident that past September. As I listened to his stories of contact with her, I found myself admiring the way he handled her departure with grace and strength. I was astonished at his daughter's ability to connect with him after her death through numerous signs.

Instantly, I recalled the grim message I'd received at the time of Chris's birth. Frank discussions with my friend about his experiences and feelings over his daughter's death forced me to examine how I might feel and react if one of my children suddenly crossed over. My heart sank at the thought and I prayed, "Please, God, not my Chris."

Six weeks later, my son was gone. My chance meeting with this man was not chance at all but was instead, I believe, a skillful and deliberate connection by God. I was being prepared. I was also correct in predicting the spiritual light in which I would view my son's death. Nevertheless, I could have had no way of knowing the level of physical and emotional pain I would experience after that death had actually occurred.

Beneath the heart-wrenching anguish of my grief, I clung to my *knowing* that we survive death with sheer determination. As I moved through my grief journey, I focused every ounce of my being on making a connection with Chris. How else could I survive his death without embracing the knowledge that we are eternal beings and that he was not gone after all? How else could I find a way to forgive myself for not being able to prevent his death unless I set out to prove there was a divine plan, and that he continued to live on after the physical demise of his body?

Looking back, I recalled the signs and hints along the way that prepared me for my child's departure. I wondered if these signs were a coincidence. Was I imagining this, or had other parents also experienced the *knowing* or precognition that their child would die young?

My experience was more common than I thought and I soon met other mothers who had known intuitively that their child would leave early. Many of these mothers had also received signs afterward that their child was still present. Like Chris, a large number of these deceased children had forewarned their parents and arranged for their early departure.

Vicky

After posting a question on Facebook to mothers about signs that their children would die young, I received a number of responses, one of which came from Vicky Edgerly Ellis. She says:

> When my son was five days old, I knew that he would "die young." It was around two o'clock AM when my husband and daughter were sound asleep and I had just nursed my son and put him back to bed. While standing over his crib in that quiet time of the morning I just *knew*. I remember feeling it as if it had just happened and it took my breath away.
>
> It was sort of like a "dream" for the next eighteen years. I would think of it occasionally but then just set it aside. When he was a young boy he was very accident prone. We had many trips to the hospital ER for stitches and casts and such.

I would always breathe a sigh of relief when he came away from these accidents with his life still intact.

I did not expect, however, the news that he had hung himself on Mother's Day 2002. He was eighteen years old. But once I heard the news, I just sort of exhaled, hung my head and thought, 'well, now it's done'.

Even in the early days [of my grief journey] I could feel grateful and honored that he called me before he did it and wished me a happy Mother's Day and told me he loved me. To this day I enjoy watching for the signs he leaves me every year on Mother's Day. Some of the signs are very strange and creative and even make me laugh!

Nancy

Through the miracle of Spirit, I met a remarkable woman named Nancy Myers, author of *Entering the Light Fantastic: Discovering Life After Life Through Orbs.* Her beautiful son, Robbie, died in January 2010. While away on a trip and suffering from a bad cold, he accidently mixed several types of cold medicine, alcohol and his prescription painkiller for a back injury. We talked about our boys and the circumstances surrounding their deaths. She also knew her son would die young. Nancy says:

> Deep in my soul I always knew that I would not have Robbie for a long time and I knew he was going to be twice the age of my brother, Craig, when he died. My brother crossed over just before his fourteenth birthday and Robbie left just before his twenty-eighth birthday. I don't know why I *knew* this; I just did. Maybe Spirit let me remember just that much to help prepare me.
>
> When Robbie walked out the door to travel back East to be with his cousins for three days, I knew that it was the last time I would see him. I woke up right at the time he crossed and I knew when the phone rang at six in the morning that

it was my brother-in-law calling to give me the news. I didn't want to answer it.

This was confirmed in a dream when Craig and Robbie "visited" me together in an ADC. A medium, Rebecca Rosen, also told me they were together and were in the same soul family.

Robbie, I think, knew something but he didn't want to upset me. He was very spiritual and philosophical about things, reading books, listening to *Coast to Coast* radio, etc., searching for answers.

I asked Nancy how knowing that her son was going to cross early had helped her through the grieving process of coping with her loss. She responded:

As you are sadly acquainted with the gut-wrenching emotions we parents feel when we lose a child, it sucks the life out of us and for a while there is only sadness. With me, however, there was always (right from the first minute I received the news) a voice in my head, no, my heart, that said, "Remember. You knew this is what was going to happen and now you must learn or remember why."

Then, with my son's help from the other side, my spiritual purpose began revealing itself and I learned that my purpose was inextricably tied into my son's life-after-life. The whole purpose for his sacrifice was to help teach others. This is something he agreed to do. Believing this, which I do with every fiber of my being, how then could I remain in a state of despair?

A much bigger picture began to come into focus. This wasn't about me, and this is hard, but I had to look past how Robbie's crossing affected just me, his mother. This loss and the lessons were for the greater good of all and I had to do

> everything in my power to honor my son's life purpose. It carries me through every day.
>
> Don't get me wrong, I still miss his physical presence, his hugs, his smiles, his humor, and once in awhile I sit in a corner and cry. We have to let that out. Then I pull myself together and remember our purpose and the important work we have to do.
>
> Robbie validated my feelings when he relayed messages through a very accurate medium who said that Robbie sends me dragonflies as a sign that he is nearby. I never really noticed them before, but big orange ones have begun to show up, circle around me, and hover just at eye level.
>
> I can't help but notice them. I know it is more than just a coincidence when I see dragonflies out of season or at unusual times. The feeling that Robbie is behind it is just too strong to ignore and yet, this simple sign brings me such comfort to know he is nearby and it helps to carry me forward on my healing journey.

It was incredible that Nancy's experience could be so similar to mine. We each had a *knowing* of our sons' early departures and a premonition of their death within hours to days of their deaths. We both felt their crossing was for a greater purpose and felt strongly that we needed to step beyond our own pain for the greater good.

Cheryl

In February 2011, a hit and run drunk driver struck Cheryl Hammond's nineteen-year-old daughter Jessica. She died two days later. Cheryl says:

> Since Jessica's birth, I have had a gut feeling, *a knowing,* that I wouldn't have her long. I have also had repeated dreams throughout her life of being at her funeral (not surprisingly, everything at her real funeral was the same as my dreams;

the flowers, the casket, everything). Additionally, I would just get these sudden thoughts, *knowings*, or guidance (whatever you want to call it) that I was going to lose her. I had never had any of these thoughts about my other three children; it was always Jessica.

Several months before she died, my husband and I were talking and imagining what all our kids would be like when they were older. We could imagine all of them older, even our nine-year-old, but not Jessica. About a month before she died, I just got this overwhelming *knowing* and I said to my husband, "It's like Jesse has learned all she needs to know and doesn't need to be here anymore."

As for Jessica, she just seemed in a hurry to get everything done. Her life was jam packed with experiences. She was the most altruistic, compassionate, adventurous, loving, level headed, but also free spirited person I have ever known.

She started talking about her dying as a teenager. Not in a morbid, scary way, just matter of fact. We must have had at least forty conversations about what she wanted done if she died. She would say, "Okay, Mom, if I die." Then she would proceed to tell me what she wanted done with her body, what she wanted on her headstone, what music she wanted played, what she wanted done if she was on life support, that she wanted to be an organ donor etc...I promised. Ironically, it made it so much easier.

I didn't have to make any decisions at the hospital when she was on life support or about organ donation because I *knew* what she wanted. I also didn't have to make decisions about what she would want at her funeral because I already *knew*. She spared me from having to make so many difficult decisions.

Two days before she was hit by the car, her last Facebook entry said, "I am so ready to get on the first plane to anywhere." Our last conversation was quite a sign as well. I was rushing to get out of the house the evening before it happened to take my youngest son to karate. Jessica stopped me and really wanted to talk. I was in a hurry, but saw how serious she was.

She said that she had been flipping TV channels and came across an episode of Dr. Phil or Oprah, I can't remember which one, and neither is anything she would *ever* normally watch. She said it was about parents who lose a child and how difficult it was for them. We ended up sitting down and talking about it for fifteen minutes, even though I was late. It was the last conversation I had with her. She was hit by a car the next morning.

My grief journey has been complicated though due to the violent, sudden nature of the loss. It took some time to deal with my anger at the man who killed her and at God, but I believe that Jessica and I also had a soul contract. It took some time for me to trust the messages I was receiving from Jessica after her death, but I kept hearing from her, "We are a team, Mom. We are here to make a difference. I couldn't have done it without you and you couldn't have done it without me."

Scarlett

Scarlett Lewis is the author of *Nurturing, Healing, Love: A Mother's Journey of Hope and Forgiveness*.[5] She is the mother of six-year-old Jesse Lewis, a first grader killed during the assault at Sandy Hook Elementary School in December 2012. Jesse faced his attacker head on and when either his gun jammed or he stopped to reload, Jesse screamed to his classmates to run. His act of selflessness and bravery saved nine precious lives before the gunman killed him.

On the day of her son's birth, Scarlett said a prayer and thanked Jesus for the beautiful gift of her son. She said, "…I know you could take him from me at any time, but please don't." She said this prayer every day of his life. As she looked back on Jesse's death, she realized that it was "just one of the countless signs that God sent to prepare me for the unimaginably painful event in my future."[6] Scarlett knew that she wouldn't have Jesse long and that God would call him home early.

She also mentions Jesse had questioned his father, Neil, a week before the shooting, about his grandmother and how he would be able to recognize her in Heaven if he died. After the shooting, his father pointed out that Jesse had crossed over on the same day his mother had five years earlier.

Both Scarlett and Neil were supposed to meet in Jesse's classroom that afternoon, but Jesse was convinced it wasn't going to happen. Both Scarlett and Neil felt that Jesse's reaction was unusual. Then as Neil dropped Jesse off at school and said good-bye that fateful morning, Jesse put his hands on his dad's shoulders and said, "I just want you to know… it's going to be okay. And that I love you and mom."[7]

A week after the shooting, Scarlett received a box of Jesse's personal things from his classroom. As she carefully sorted through the items, she came across a penciled drawing dated just days before the shooting. It was a picture of a smiling little boy with angel wings standing across from a taller menacing figure. Jesse had obliterated its face with black scribbling. It was clear to Scarlett what the picture represented. She knew *"that Jesse had spiritual knowledge of what was to be, and that he himself was part of God's bigger master plan."*[8]

It seems Jesse knew on a soul level that something was going to happen and he was preparing for his crossing. Even Scarlett knew on a deep level at his birth she would not have Jesse long. As she says, "Jesse was born brave. I am now certain he was put on this Earth to save lives."[9]

Once Jesse crossed over, he began to communicate with his mother and many other people through ADC's, letting them know he was still very much present. Jesse's communication began the morning after the shooting with an unmistakable flickering of lights for Scarlett. She knew it was from Jesse and it immediately relieved her gut wrenching pain of remembering her little boy was gone.

Relatives reported feeling and hearing Jesse nearby. They would also wake at three o'clock AM with a strong feeling of Jesse's presence. Scarlett watched words erase themselves from her computer screen. She felt Jesse brush her cheek. His toys would appear from nowhere. While flying to Disney World the in-flight music selection kept changing channels, either to a favorite of Jesse's or to songs with lyrics that expressed Scarlett's feelings. There were signs everywhere that told Scarlett and her family that Jesse was still with them, albeit in another form.

At one point, I cried as I read her story, flooded with relief and validation that someone else had experienced the beautiful after-death communication possible with our loved ones. I wasn't imagining the synchronicities, *knowings*, or ADC's. I knew Chris's death was part of a divine plan. Scarlett also recognized the signs as part of a much larger plan from God too.

Why did Scarlett *know* at Jesse's birth that she wouldn't have her son long or Jesse prepare for his crossing unless it was a plan made ahead of time? Why did he draw that picture? Was it a clue for his mother and those left behind that he was part of a much grander plan? What urged him to ask about recognizing his grandmother in Heaven, or feel so certain that his parents weren't going to meet him that afternoon? Why did he tell his father it would all be okay, unless he knew on a soul level he was preparing to cross over?

Mary

Dr. Mary Neal, author of the New York Times bestseller, *To Heaven and Back: A Doctor's Extraordinary Account of her Death, Heaven, Angels, and Life Again*, recounts her near-death experience (NDE) from a kayaking accident.[10]

However, it was not Mary's NDE that caught my attention; it was her son's death and the circumstances surrounding it. In her book,

Mary describes her son, Willie, as a young child of four or five, who says he would not live past age eighteen. He also reminds his mother that she knew of the plan.[11] Just before his accident at age nineteen, Willie made several unusual preparations for his crossing.

These preparations included a discussion of his burial plans, life insurance policy and will, which was unusual for a healthy nineteen-year-old. Then one day, as he and his roller skiing[12] companion crested a hill with a breathtaking view, Willie said, "If we died, wouldn't this be an incredible last vision?" Three minutes later, he was gone. A young man who was distracted while driving hit Willie.[13]

She also says, "Before Willie's eighteenth birthday, I had a dream in which a boy whom I did not know told me he had traded places with Willie." She discovered later that afternoon that that day before a young man in her community died on his way to an athletic event. She felt compassion for him and his family and wondered if that meant Willie would be spared. As it turned out, Willie lived one more year.[14]

How did Willie know he was going to die early? Why did he tell his mother she knew of the plan? Why did Mary have that dream? Why did Willie discuss his burial plans, or say those haunting words minutes before his death, unless there really was a divine plan and something beyond this life as a human?

Vicky Edgerly Ellis, Nancy Myers, Cheryl Hammond, Scarlett Lewis and Dr. Mary Neal's experiences validated my thoughts, feelings and experiences with my son. There was strength in numbers. Their stories gave me hope that there really was a divine plan and I wasn't imagining my *knowing* and the premonitions I had of my son's death as a symptom of my grief. Was this type of experience limited to parents' premonitions of their child's death?

Ari

Recently, I came across a story of a young girl who not only had a premonition of her parent's death; she traveled to Heaven with them when they died. Ari Hallmark is a near-death experiencer and the co-author of *To Heaven: After the Storm*.[15] She had a premonition at age six. In November of 2010, she had a dream and *knew* her parents were going to die. All she wanted to do was spend time with them before they left. Ari began to sob at kindergarten. Her teacher said it wasn't ordinary crying and it continued for two months.

Neither she nor the children could get her to stop. The teacher tried everything to comfort her. Neither the counselor, nurse nor her parents could console her. Ari's behavior was uncharacteristic and nothing could change her insistence she *knew* both her parents were going to die. She eventually stopped crying when her parents bribed her with an upcoming family trip after her mother's graduation from nursing school.[16]

On April 27, 2011, an EF4 tornado struck and hit Ari and her family. Ari's parents, grandparents and little cousin died. Ari was thrown two hundred yards—the length of two football fields. She survived, but spent three days in intensive care with broken bones, staples and seventy stitches in her back. Ari had a near-death experience and traveled to Heaven with her entire family. She saw they were all okay. Ari even saw Jesus holding her baby cousin and her grandfather who had previously crossed over.

While her family passed through the doors into Heaven, Ari wasn't allowed to stay and was escorted back to Earth by an angel with long blond hair. With the help of her teacher and her grief counselor, Ari has co-written a book to help comfort other parents and children who have lost loved ones so that they may understand that there truly is something more beyond this life.

How did Ari know her parents were going to die months ahead of time? Was this a pre-birth contract? Where did this information, this *knowing*, come from? Why did she get to travel with her family and see them delivered safely to Heaven? Was it another clue to the eternal nature of the soul and life after death?

Jeff

Jeff Olsen and I met at the National IANDS Conference in 2013. He is an inspirational speaker and the author of *I Knew Their Hearts*.[17] Jeff was at the wheel when his car flipped, killing his wife Tamara, toddler son Griffin, and injuring his older son Spencer. Jeff sustained life-threatening injuries and spent several pain-filled months in the hospital recovering.

The doctors had never seen someone with his injuries survive. He endured multiple surgeries and had his left leg amputated above the knee. Jeff also had a profound near-death experience during the accident. When Jeff looked back on the events leading up to the accident, he also discovered signs and hints of his wife's crossing. He says:

> The morning of our family trip to visit Tamara's parents for Easter, Tamara said, "I had the weirdest dream last night. I dreamed you were marrying someone else...It was really weird because I was okay with it. There I was, watching you marry another woman, and I was at peace. In fact, I felt content."
>
> It didn't make sense to me at the time as we loved each other deeply and were more excited about our lives now than we had ever been. The day after Easter, after we said our goodbyes and were all loaded in the car, I was surprised when Tamara insisted that I wait while she returned to the house to say good-bye yet again."[18]

During the four-hour drive home their SUV rolled, killing Tamara and their infant son Griffin. Years later, Jeff found love and married again. What caused Tamara to have that dream days before her death and yet be at peace with the notion that her husband would marry again? Why did she insist on one last good-bye with her parents? Did Tamara somehow know on a soul level of her impending crossing?

Tom

Tom Zuba is the author of *Permission to Mourn: A New Way to Do Grief* and has experienced the deaths of his young daughter, son and his wife in three separate events. During our interview, he said:

> My wife Trici was a perfectly healthy forty-three-year-old woman in the prime of her life who was eager to have one more child. We had a booming business, we were contemplating buying a new house, and all systems were go. Two weeks before Christmas, she said, "Tom, there are two songs I want played at my funeral, "Go Lassie Go" and "Come Oh Come Emanuel." I know "Come Oh Come Emanuel" is a Christmas song but even if I die in the summer, those are the two songs I want."
>
> I said what I have always said, "Don't tell me because I am going first." Two days after Christmas, she said the same thing. "I'm serious, Tom. Those are the two songs I want played at my funeral."
>
> For Christmas that year, she gave me a stone with a Celtic symbol on it and when I turned it over it said *Journey*. She gave me a mouse pad with a picture of me and our two sons. She was not in the picture. She also gave me a book of Irish Christmas stories. The inscription said, *Dear Tom, Thank you for giving me everything I ever wanted and giving it to me all over again.*
>
> A week later, I was planning her funeral, eight years after the death of our eighteen-month old daughter, Erin. I realized the gift she gave me was "don't have any regrets." A huge shift occurred for me. There was a much deeper *knowing* and there was a yearning for and understanding of what just happened. Her death was so explosive and so unbelievable I realized this wasn't random.

This is exactly what I thought about my son's death. It wasn't random. There was purpose and meaning behind Chris's death. Did that mean there was a plan of some sort, possibly a pre-birth plan in which we all agreed to these experiences?

CHAPTER FOUR

"Your actions, in passing, pass not away,
for every good work is a grain of seed for eternal life."
~ Bernard of Clairvaux

Pre-Birth Contracts

Helen

As I began to explore our connection to an afterlife and a pre-birth plan, I came across the book, *Testimony of Light: An Extraordinary Message of Life After Death*. Author Helen Greaves channels Francis Banks, a close friend with whom she spent the last eight years of her life.[19] During the time the two worked together both psychically and spiritually, they also explored deep levels of meditation.

Francis Banks spent twenty-five years as a Sister in the Anglican Community of the Resurrection in South Africa. Banks also received her master's degree in psychology from Rhodes University and was an author of many books on the subject. Francis transitioned in November of 1965. Francis says from the other side:

> I am becoming increasingly aware of a Pattern and a Plan. The Blueprint of one's efforts, one's successes and failures on all the planes; material, emotional, mental, and spiritual does indicate that a definite line of advance is voluntarily accepted by the soul *before incarnation*.

...Therefore, up to a point, it fixes its own "coming events" because they will afford it the necessary experience it has come to gather and these will be commensurate with the overall Pattern associated with its progress.[20]

Betty

After reading about Frances, I remembered a woman named Betty Eadie, author of the *New York Times* bestseller, *Embraced by the Light*.[21] Betty's near-death experience occurred in her hospital room after an operation. During her NDE, she was shown souls in Heaven choosing their birth parents and even the circumstances, challenges, and blessings surrounding their birth, ensuing life and death. Whether they were born with a handicap, contracted an illness, including cancer, or died young, they all had prearranged these experiences for their soul growth and that of their family members.

Also during her trip to Heaven, one young woman in particular captured her attention. She was filled with energy and joy. Betty recognized her and the love they felt for each other. She knew she would always remember her.

Betty saw the mission she had to complete on Earth and was strongly encouraged to return. Back in her body in the hospital room, an angelic toddler with a halo of glowing light visited her. The toddler was drawn to Betty's husband Joe, although Joe couldn't see her. The little girl danced around the room, stood on the toe of his shoe and struck a ballerina pose. The toddler filled with joy!

Years later, Betty provided foster care for an infant girl until she was placed with relatives. She deeply loved this baby. Broken-hearted, Betty prayed for her return. One night a divine messenger visited Betty and told her the baby would return to her shortly.

Two weeks later, the call came and the baby returned to Betty and her family. During the time she had spent with her relatives, the infant had been severely abused and traumatized. It was a long recovery but by the time she was two and a half, she had healed. Betty and her husband adopted the little girl. Then one afternoon, Betty watched her daughter as she stood on the tip of her husband's shoe and struck the same ballerina pose she had seen the angelic toddler do in the hospital so many years before.

She recognized the spirit of the young woman she saw in Heaven as the angelic toddler she had seen in the hospital room who was now her newly adopted daughter. They were one in the same. Betty now understood why she had felt so connected to the fostered infant and why it was so important she return from Heaven during her NDE and become this child's mother. She was needed back on Earth to provide the love and nurturing to help heal this precious child as she incarnated on Earth to complete her own mission.

As a mother in grief, I found myself comforted by Betty's knowledge of her pre-birth contract and her experience with the little girl whose spirit she had met in Heaven. It filled me with hope that I had also known my son's spirit in Heaven, and that we were both part of a grander plan. The following two stories from RaNelle and Nicola also jogged my memory of yet another piece to God's grand plan.

RaNelle

Severely burned in a plane crash, RaNelle Wallace, co-author of *The Burning Within,* suffered a near-death experience caused by her injuries.[22] During her NDE in Heaven, she met her grandmother who told her she must go back. She said RaNelle's children needed her and she still had much to accomplish. Upon viewing her burned body and the pain she would endure if she returned, RaNelle refused.

Suddenly her "grandmother swept open her arms and commanded, 'Look.' A rift opened in space before us, and I saw a young man walking toward us. At first, he seemed not to understand why he was there. Then he recognized me and looked stunned…His name was Nathaniel. He had not yet been born on Earth."[23]

RaNelle realized she would be this young man's mother. She knew that she must return in order for him to be born to complete his earthly mission. Years later, and moments before the birth of a baby boy, the same young man she had seen in Heaven during her NDE appeared to her right in the delivery room. As he mouthed the words "thank you," RaNelle felt a wave of love brush over her. Just as he disappeared, she delivered her son and named him Nathaniel.

After reading about these near-death experiences, I can imagine that some might be inclined to think they are far-fetched and impossible, fantasies even, but when combined with real experiences from non-NDErs, they begin to take on an entirely new significance.

Julia Assante, Ph.D., author of *The Last Frontier: Exploring the Afterlife and Transforming our Fear of Death* is also a psychic and a medium. During my interview with Julia, she said often times she can see children who have picked their parents hovering around them waiting to be born.

> They usually appear around the age of four. By that, I mean they appear identifiable. If they appeared as an infant or neonate, you couldn't distinguish one from another. They can have the maturity of a full-grown adult. They can be very demanding.
>
> They can take over an entire session and they can be very explicit in what they need to get from their parents and what their parents have to do to make themselves ready. Sometimes their parents are unable to have them, so they often come into somebody on the same street so they grow up near the family.

Nicola

The following story appears to validate Julia's experiences with pre-born children. I discovered Nicola's story during my research on pre-birth contracts. Jeffrey Long, M.D., is the author of the New York Times Bestseller *Evidence of the Afterlife: The Science of Near-Death Experiences*. He is a radiation oncologist who has created the website NDERF.org. or Near-Death Experience Research Foundation. It is one of the largest comprehensive websites on NDEs. Nicola writes:

My friend and I met as schoolteachers at the same school, several years ago. She was pregnant when we met, and she chose me to be present at the birth of her child, because she was a single mother and afraid of being alone. It was a tremendous honor to be invited into the delivery room because, even though I have children of my own, it was a fascinating opportunity to see a birth without experiencing the pain myself!

My friend delivered a baby boy named Michael, and it was an incredible experience. Tragically, my friend passed away suddenly, just months after her son was born. He has been raised by her parents ever since. The boy now goes to the school where his mother and I taught, and this year he is in my 4th Grade class, nine years after his birth and mother's passing.

It is with a heavy heart that I teach him each day. I have never told him that I was there for his birth because I didn't want the other students to think that he had special treatment, and I didn't want to upset him with thoughts of his mother. Perhaps his grandparents told him that I was there, but I'm not sure. He does know, however, that his mom and I were friends.

I was speaking with my class about our memories for a poetry writing assignment. I asked them to think back to the earliest memories they have. Most students talked about Kindergarten, or perhaps day care, or vague memories of old toys, etc from three or four-years-old.

Michael put up his hand and said that he remembers watching everyone from up in the sky, and being in his mother's belly before he was born. He said that when he was waiting to be born, he was invisible and he was in my grey car with me on the way to the hospital while I listened to the song "Winter Spring Summer or Fall." This is what he called the song. He likely doesn't know the real name, and he probably hasn't heard it since...but it was "You've Got a Friend" by James Taylor. I used to have the cassette tape in that car!

This is bizarre because I did drive a grey car at that time and I haven't had one for the past seven years, two years after he was born. I can't imagine he even knows that song from today's radio music. My heart started to beat like crazy. How in the heck would he know that? Even his grandparents wouldn't have known that and his mom wouldn't have known that before she died. Even if somehow she did, he was only three-months-old when she passed. How would she tell him? I certainly never told her what song was on in my car on the way to the hospital so I can't explain this!

Michael said that he remembers me stopping for gas and asking the attendant for directions to the hospital. He said that he wanted me for his mommy because he liked my voice when I was speaking to the attendant. I did stop for gas and I was kind of lost going to a rural hospital, so I asked for directions.

Then he said that he remembers that the parking lot was partially closed for construction, so I had to park on a corner and run to the hospital. By this point, my jaw was almost on the floor and the whole class was staring at me. I had never even told the class or Michael that I was at his birth. The class must have thought this was one crazy story.

Michael then said the most incredible thing—He said that while his "real mom" was in labor, he asked God if I could be his mom because he knew that his "real mom" wouldn't survive very long, and he was afraid of being alone on Earth. Apparently, he was told that he couldn't have me for his "real mom," but that everything would be okay and he would still get to be around me during his life.

Michael said that he kept begging God for me to be his mother. He watched me go down the hallway from the birthing suite to the waiting lounge to make a phone call from a pay phone. It's true–there was no cell signal in the hospital–and that while I was there I was very cold so I put on a sweater that someone else had left on one of the waiting room chairs.

By this point, the hairs on the back of my neck were standing up. I hate to admit this, but I did find a nice warm cardigan in that waiting room and I put it on because I was so cold. I've never done anything like that before, but it was a small hospital and there were literally no other people in the labor ward and I waited to see if anyone would come to claim the sweater, and no one did. I was so cold! I put it on and ended up wearing it home.

Shame on me, I know, I still feel guilty about that. I've felt so guilty that I never wore it again, especially because it reminds me of my friend who ended up passing away. Regardless, I have to mention it because I've never told anyone about taking someone else's sweater, and it's a huge part of this story!

Michael concluded by saying that he watched me make the phone call and put on the other person's sweater, and that's the last thing he remembers. He was born about thirty minutes after I went to the lounge and made that phone call.

Later, I privately said to Michael, "Yes, I was at your birth. How did you know all of that stuff?" His grandparents weren't at the birth and there was literally no way he would have known any of that. How could he make it up? He said that it's easy, he just had to think back to his earliest memories. He asked me why I don't remember being born, too and he said "It's okay, my life did turn out okay. So don't worry about not being my mom."

Wow. I write this in all sincerity as my evidence that there must be some kind of heaven up there if he could have memories of watching his birth and waiting to be born. I considered the idea that his mom speaks to him from the afterlife, and maybe she told him herself but how would she even know this information? [24]

Kristin

Both RaNelle's and Nicola's story stirred memories of my oldest daughter Kristin and her story of waiting to be delivered. As a little girl, she told me she remembered floating on the ceiling in the delivery room. She remembered being inside my body and feeling the contractions, although she didn't know what they were called. She was so confused about what was happening. She then remembered feeling a calm and loving energy explain to her that she was being born.

At that moment, she felt much safer and more willing to leave the womb naturally. Suddenly, she felt a sharp pain on her head that was too much to bear. She popped out of her body and floated above the scene. The doctor had used forceps to help deliver her. The moment she was delivered, she remembered being sucked back into her body. Then she recalled feeling very cold and placed on something hard. This was her last memory of birth.

Kristin also said she remembered being in Heaven and picking her dad and me as her parents. She told me that I was a given, but the man who would be her dad was up in the air. She had more than one choice and vaguely remembered a spirit guide suggesting her father because it would help with certain "lessons." Kristin doesn't remember whether those lessons were supposed to be for her or her father.

During Betty Eadie's near-death experience, she saw "one male spirit trying to get a mortal man and woman together on Earth—his future parents…coaching them, speaking to them, and persuading them."[25] She also mentions that we "desire to come here…to develop attributes we lack…we look upon life as a school."[26]

Kristin also remembered that while in Heaven an angel or guide sat or knelt on her right. She also remembered talking with someone her age to the left of her and said, "I will see you soon." She then recalls descending to Earth and leaving that spirit behind.

At the time Kristin mentioned all this, I didn't give her story much credence because I didn't know these kinds of experiences were possible. After reading about RaNelle and Nathaniel, Betty and her adopted daughter, and Nicola and Michael, I realized that Kristin's experience was real.

If that were true, then it was possible that her brother Chris had a pre-birth plan, an agreement with me, and had also simply left his body at the time of his accident, just as Kristin had left her body during her difficult birth. If all these things were true, then it was possible that Chris was alive and well in Spirit, which would validate the *knowing* I had during the initial phone call from my brother that he was safe and he was home.

During Dr. Mary Neal's recovery from her kayaking accident and near-death experience, she would have intermittent visits with an angel. The angel talked about the opportunity and privilege to come to Earth and how God creates our "life design." She learned that we review our life design with our "personal planning angel."

We make a basic outline for our life that includes definite times when we can choose to exit and return to God.[27] Sometimes we receive new missions to undertake. We are guided to these exit points or missions by our own consciousness or by "angelic intervention." The angel reminded Mary that when the time came for her son's death she needed to be "a rock of support" for her family and community.

Not until after her son's death did Mary have the opportunity to review these different events and realized his passing must have been pre-planned. The fact that she was alerted to her son's early death when he was young and reminded about it from an angel after her NDE, encouraged her to stand in a place of strength when he died and help her family move through the grief process.

Tom

Tom Zuba, author of *Permission to Mourn: A New Way to Do Grief* experienced the deaths of his young daughter, son and his wife in three separate events. Impressed by his ability to embrace joy and happiness in his life after three tragedies, I interviewed Tom for my documentary about healing grief. He says:

> Eight years after the unexpected death of my eighteen-month-old daughter, Erin, my wife, Trici, died suddenly. A few weeks before she died, I read the book *The Seat of the Soul* by Gary Zukav. There was a passage in the book that speaks to the fact that when a child dies we don't know what contracts have been made or what healing has been served. That really resonated with me and spoke to me so deeply.
>
> When my wife died just a few weeks later, I thought, well if contracts have been made between Erin, Trici and me regarding Erin's death, then surely contracts have been made between Trici and me regarding her death. We also had two sons, Rory and Sean, so I knew that contracts had been made throughout the entire family and that helped me look at Trici's death very, very differently.

These stories were further validation that the *knowing*, forewarning and synchronistic events surrounding my son's death came from some place outside of me. They helped to ease my pain and deepen my understanding of death and our roles as eternal beings. They also gave me hope that there really was meaning and purpose to my son's death and his motorcycle accident was *not* a random event.

Throughout my life, I have been reminded of our connection to Spirit. When Christopher died, I had no other option except to view my son's death as an opportunity to prove to myself what I had known since childhood: *that we don't die*. Now, with someone I knew and loved on the other side, I was compelled to step beyond my pain for the greater good and put my theory, my *knowing*, to the test.

Was there really life after death as I had always believed? Betty Eadie saw her adopted daughter during her NDE and years before her appearance in her life. RaNelle Wallace encountered her unborn son during her NDE and returned to life to see him appear in the delivery room moments before her baby boy was born. Young Michael described events moments before his birth to Nicola that were impossible for him to know.

Even my daughter Kristin spoke of her experience in the delivery room and her time in Heaven when she chose both her father and me as her parents. In Chapter Three, Dr. Mary Neal's son told her of his early death and that she had agreed to the plan. She was also told by an angel that we make a basic outline for our life with different intersections of time at which we can choose to exit and return to God.

Many of the mothers I have spoken with who have lost children report that as they look back on their child's life, they received messages of their child's early passing, or the children themselves stated the approximate time of their passing.

After reading about the pre-birth plans and experiences, I wondered how many parents might benefit from a gentle conversation to spark a memory or experience that may alert them to signs or clues of their child's pre-birth plan and thus aid in their bereavement healing.

These stories reinforced my own intuition and experiences and caused me to conclude that a human has at least two parts: a body and a soul. The body may die but the soul survives, with memories and consciousness intact.

For the first time since my son's death, I began to open to the possibility of forgiving myself and releasing the guilt I felt. I began to see a much larger picture and the possibility that there was a divine plan for my son's death, moreover, that both he and I had known about it.

Vicky Edgerly Ellis, Nancy Myers, Cheryl Hammond, Scarlett Lewis, Mary Neal and I all knew our children would cross before we did. Our children knew it too. Ari knew her parents were going to die and both Tom and Jeff's wives had premonitions of their impending crossings. How then could we have obtained this information if not for our participation in a plan prior to our births? These experiences all meant that I was on the right track and my inner guidance was correct.

There was something more.

During this time, I continued to receive after-death communications from my son that lifted me up during my grief. Then twenty months after Chris's death another clue to our identity as eternal beings suddenly appeared.

CHAPTER FIVE

"The real voyage of discovery consists not in seeking new landscapes but in having new eyes."
~ Marcel Proust

The Light Being

Late one night I awoke shivering. A chill had descended in the high desert of Southern California where I lived. I slipped from my bed to turn off the air conditioner and as I stepped back into my darkened bedroom, I froze. A brilliant ball of white light, slightly larger than a ping-pong ball, was hovering before me in mid-air.

The light also seemed startled. After a momentary hesitation, it darted to my left, parallel to the wall in front of me, took a sharp left and followed that wall for about five feet before it disappeared. It left a trail of light much like a twirling Fourth of July sparkler.

My mind raced. Was there a burglar with a flashlight outside my sliding door? I bolted and ran through the house to check the locks. After I rechecked my alarm system, I rushed to my young daughter's bedside. She was sleeping soundly and I cautiously crept back to my bed; my senses hyper-alert.

Terrified, I drew the cold covers to my chin, shivering now for a different reason. I lay there wide-eyed in the dark, my heart still pounding as I listened for the slightest sound that could indicate an intruder. I tried to find a logical explanation for what I'd seen but could find none and my mind filled with frightening scenarios.

After I'd calmed down and was able to reason with myself, I realized the burglar scenario didn't ring true. I have blackout curtains on my windows and the light had started on a solid wall next to the sliding door. It would be impossible for a simple flashlight to penetrate the wall and create the bright white ball of light I'd seen hovering approximately three feet down from the ceiling and three feet out from the wall.

Then I considered something of a different nature. Could the ball of light have been a spiritual event: a light from God? Was it a new kind of ADC or after-death communication? Was it an angel, or better yet, did it have something to do with my son Chris?

The following morning I called a girlfriend and described what I'd witnessed the night before.

She simply said, "That was a light being."

"What's that?"

"A light being can be any number of things," she answered, "including an emanation from Spirit, an inter-dimensional being, our guides and angels, an extraterrestrial, or a sentient being. Who really knows for sure? But they are here to help us."

She told me that the International Orb and Light Being Conference scheduled at the Palm Springs Convention Center, was just a few weeks away.

"Are you kidding me?" I asked as I rolled my eyes. "An orb convention?"

The word "orb" is generally used to describe a ball of light seen in digital photos. They can appear as a sphere of light, circle of light, oval of light, ball of light, disc of light, and being of light. They have also been referred to in the near-death experiences as "globular or egg-shaped spheres of some sort."[28] I knew what an orb was but I hadn't heard the term "light being."

Orbs appeared in my photographs off and on for several years, but this was the first time I had seen one with my eyes. As I pondered the identity and meaning of "light being," I wondered again if it had anything to do with my son. I was a grieving parent. Was I onto valuable information, or just grasping for anything to make sense of my painful loss?

Photo 1 © Virginia Hummel. A single bright orb in my kitchen.

If I saw this "light being" with my eyes, there must be a reason. Through the years, I've learned that nothing is a coincidence. Carl Jung coined the term "synchronicity." He used it to describe the moment when the external and internal events of a person's mind seem to coincide perfectly. I believe it also describes the moment we recognize that we are divinely guided and led.

The skeptical side of me whispered that orbs in my photos were just dust or lens flare—but now I had experienced an orb first-hand. I thought orbs were an interesting phenomenon over the years, but not compelling enough to research, or spend any amount of time contemplating what they were.

After all, even if they were real, what possible meaning did they have in my life? How could they help me in my day-to-day living, with my relationships, my bills, or my job?

Yet now inner guidance or intuition was urging me to look into this phenomenon further. Was there a connection, a reason the ball of light had appeared that night, and was it important? I considered the event I had experienced in my bedroom as my personal invitation to attend the Palm Springs Conference to learn more about orbs.

Meanwhile, I discovered a few recent photos that contained orbs, taken after my son's accident when Logan, his five-year-old son, and his mother came to visit. I immediately began my research on orbs and light beings on the Internet.

There were only a handful of books on the subject at the time with varying opinions. One book, *The Orb Project*, by Míċeál Ledwith, D.D., LL.D. and Klaus Heinemann, Ph.D., provided some scientific insight into this relatively new field.[29]

A skeptic at heart, I knew the only way I would be able to learn exactly what orbs represented was to experience them for myself. I have always believed in life after death and that we are guided by Spirit if we are awake enough to recognize the signs. Yet, I didn't want to get my hopes up that orbs could in some way be connected to my son. But what if they were connected?

A memory came to mind and I recalled my older daughter Kristin mentioning what she calls "her angels" who appear to her as sparkling lights. She has seen "orbs" with her physical eyes all of her life, although she hadn't specifically used the word "orb" to describe them. As her mother, I believed her when she told me she was seeing something, yet I had a strong skeptical side that caused me to wonder if what she was seeing was real. Since I couldn't see them, a part of me didn't know if what she was describing really existed. Now I had seen one with my own eyes and I knew it was real.

Ashlee

Kristin reminded me of an experience her best friend Ashlee Yates had with a ball of light while they were in college. When I spoke with Ashlee, she said:

When we were roommates in college, I awoke one night unexpectedly. I am a deep sleeper and never wake during the night. I was occupying the bottom bunk and as I opened my eyes, across the room to my right there appeared a ball of light. It was about the size of a tennis ball and pale golden yellow in color. I blinked a few times to clear my eyes, thinking it would disappear. I wasn't terrified by its appearance, just uneasy.

I called out to Kristin to tell her what was happening. She sleepily answered that it was my guardian angel. I closed my eyes and tried to make it go away but it felt as if it wanted to be seen. When I opened my eyes, it was suddenly right in front of me. It hovered a foot from my face. I could see squiggly lines radiating out from it like a sunburst

Photo 2 © Naomi Fugiwara Orb with radiating squiggly lines.

Then I reached out to touch it and was surprised that my hand went right through it. It then faded away as if it were getting smaller and smaller. That was the first and only time I have seen it.

Ashlee's story started me thinking. I wondered if I had any more photos with orbs. As I began sifting through years of old photos, I found some pictures with orbs pre-dating Chris's death, including a picture of my son and me surrounded by these light beings.

They were intriguing, but it wasn't until the spring of 2009 that I began seriously photographing orbs. One evening the sudden urge to grab my camera overwhelmed me. I turned my flash from "auto" to "on" because I'd heard this made it easier to capture the orbs in photos. I started to take pictures and discovered my living room was filled with orbs that night.

Photo 3 © Virginia Hummel. Orbs in my kitchen.
See OrbWhisperer.com for the colored photo.

Excitedly, I called Kristin and told her about the orb photos I had just captured.

"Did you get any colored orbs?" she asked.

"They come in colors?" I dropped the phone and ran outside into the dark. My first shot captured two orbs. One was deep blue and the other was a dark golden color.

I was hooked!

The beautiful colors and numbers of orbs that began to appear in my photos were startling. I had seen photos of orbs in the few books published on the topic and on websites. The majority was taken outside in the dark. As I began to photograph them outside, I wondered if they could just as easily come inside. I learned that indeed they could. In fact, from the comfort of my living room sofa, I was getting great pictures of hundreds of orbs.

As a grieving parent, I was filled with joy and excitement each time I photographed them. I delighted in their presence yet I didn't understand why their presence had such an impact on me emotionally, and *why* I was so thrilled and comforted by their appearance. They gave me hope that I wasn't alone and there was truly something more to life than what I could see. All the while, I continued to wonder if they weren't somehow connected to my son. Were other people experiencing this same phenomenon? More importantly, were there other stories and experiences that linked orbs to the human soul?

Bob

Bob Fairchild contacted me through my website and shared a story about his orb encounter just after the death of his beloved wife. Bob writes:

> My wife and soul mate of thirty-five years passed away from colon cancer on November 5, 2012 in Kemptville, Ontario Canada. We had conversations before her cancer diagnosis about leaving signs for the other—whoever went first. It was important for each of us to know if there was something beyond death.
>
> After my wife passed, I made a deal with my two children: a daughter aged twenty-six and pregnant, and a son aged twenty-four, that we would all sleep together in my king-sized bed for a few nights, and that if anyone was awake and couldn't sleep, we would talk.
>
> It was for more my benefit than my children as I was having some problems with nighttime panic attacks, which ensued a few weeks before my wife's passing. I was only too glad to have someone to talk to. That night my son and I awoke and started talking.
>
> About thirty minutes into the conversation, we experienced an earth tremor. My senses were on high alert because of this

THE LIGHT BEING

as I continued to talk with my son. We did not want to wake my daughter as she had been through a rough day and needed her sleep. About twenty minutes after the earth tremor, I happened to notice something out of the corner of my eye.

I have lived in this house and slept in this same bedroom for twenty-seven years. It is out in the country and surrounded by a mature forest of maples and hemlock trees and far from any source of light. What I saw was a single brilliant disk of light about four inches in diameter over my wife's closet door. Our walls are dark green with white pine wainscoting. The intensity of light was consistent from the center of the disk to the edge and did not luminesce beyond the edge of the disk. The color was white with a little bit of yellow.

Following the appearance of this disk, a second one appeared which slightly overlapped the first, followed by a third and then a fourth disk: each of which overlapped the previous. The total appearance was very much like the symbol used by Audi cars with the four overlapping circles.

After the fourth circle appeared, all four circles disappeared together. The whole scene lasted about three seconds. I asked my son if he saw this but unfortunately, he had closed his eyes and was starting to doze during the interruption in our conversation.

The same event occurred later in the morning just before the sun came up, but the intensity of the light was diminished and the circles disappeared individually and not at the same time after the appearance of the fourth disk. I compared the brilliance of this light to a high intensity LED flashlight that I held close to the wall trying but unable to get that level of brilliance. There was no beam of light that emitted into our bedroom and what I saw was not from any outside source.

All I know is that I no longer have any doubt that there is something beyond death and that death is not an endpoint in our lives but a passage to something else. I am still trying to understand the meaning of this. I have no photographs but I know what I saw and it has changed the way I view life.

Touched by Bob's story and the synchronicity of the lights appearing just after his wife had passed, I was also delighted to know that I hadn't just imagined the orb in my bedroom. Could the lights we saw be related to both Bob's wife and my son? Were there other stories about a ball of light appearing during grief?

Alan

In March of 2015, I was contacted by Alan Bird who lives in Surrey, England. He shared a story similar to Bob Fairchild's story after his wife crossed over from cancer. Alan says:

> My wife died on the March 10, 2014 after a short, but immensely brave battle with late stage cervical cancer. We had been married for forty-seven years and fourteen days. Three or four weeks before her demise she said to me, "I'll never leave you Alan" and I often draw on that when my spirit is low.
>
> A couple of months after her spirit was set free, I witnessed the following events. It was around 10:30 pm and I was about to get into bed. I was standing at the foot of the bed and as I turned to get into "my" side of the bed I noticed "something white" on the floor about halfway along and at the side of the bed (the bedroom lights were off and the only light in the room was natural light from outside). My immediate thought was this is a piece of fur from my ginger and white cat but, as I took a step forward, the "something white" suddenly transformed into a spinning circle of light (about the size of a tennis ball), it was three or four inches above the carpeted floor and had other circles of light within it. The

whole "event" lasted for about five seconds and I was rooted to the spot while this was taking place.

I feel privileged to have witnessed this phenomenon and know what I would like it to be, but I haven't got a clue. Also, I have done a little reading concerning "orbs" but they have always been described as solid balls of light whereas "my orb" was "see through" and resembled an "armillary sphere."

Was Alan witnessing the 3D form of an orb with the flat concentric circles we see in a photograph?

The Reyes

Jim and Anne Reyes had a sighting in their home that they couldn't explain. Anne writes:

> My mother-in-law had died about ten days prior to this sighting. My husband Jim was sitting at the dining room table, I was standing. I turned around, looked up, and saw a perfectly white light about the size of a large dinner plate. I walked over to look and saw this opaque orb and it suddenly changed before our eyes. It looked like clouds were moving quickly through it from left to right. Then suddenly it just got small and then disappeared! We believe this had something to do with our mother's spirit.

Sandy

Christmas 2015 brought an unusual gift to Sandy Arsenault Panek and her husband, one she believes came from her son PJ who crossed over in 2011 from a boating accident.

> On December 26, 2015, my husband and I were playing bingo with our grandson. It was a rainy cold evening when I heard my front door rattle like someone was trying to enter our home, but no one came in so we ignored it. Then it

happened again. I said to my husband, "It sounds like someone is at the door. Did you hear that?"

He had heard what I had heard. I checked the front door and no one was there. But when I returned to the bingo game we were playing, I felt there was a presence around us. After my grandson left for the evening to go home with his dad, I decided to sit out on my front porch. That's when I noticed a "phosphorescent" ball of light the size of a large egg perched on the tip of a tree branch, just sitting there glowing a luminescent green.

I looked to see if it could be a star or a planet shining down, but it wasn't in the sky. The ball of light was resting on the tree branch, just glowing. I tapped on my bay window to get my husband's attention to signal for him to have a look. He quickly came out and was witnessing the same phenomenon with me. He went to get his binoculars to have a closer look. It was a glowing ball sitting in the tree. No evidence of any glow bugs in that ball of light.

I looked up phosphorus light emitting from plants, but it only had scientific explanations about a plant glowing. The whole tree wasn't glowing. Phosphorus lights only glow in warmer temperatures. It was not warm out last night.

Could this have been a visit from my deceased son? First the door rattling, then the feeling of a presence then the glowing ball of light? I would like to believe we had a visit from him. This morning I went outside and took my binoculars out. There is no evidence of a firefly nest. There was nothing there today to explain what we saw.

These stories validated what my intuition had already told me; the balls of light or orbs were in some way connected to Spirit and our loved ones. Now I needed to prove this supposition through investigation and research.

If I could prove what my intuition was telling me, then I wouldn't be separated from my son: I would know that he still lives on. Next to having Chris back in the flesh, this would be the greatest comfort I could experience.

Each night, I started with the same routine of taking orb photos. From that time on, orbs became a daily part of my life. They were on my mind from the moment I woke up until I fell asleep. I talked about them constantly and spent hours on the Internet in search of photos, stories and information about this phenomenon.

Almost on a daily basis, I experienced a connection to Spirit, whether it was through orbs or after-death communication (ADCs). Yet in spite of these amazing experiences, the skeptical part of me continued to question if what I was experiencing was real or merely a symptom of my grief.

Was I creating this myth myself about this spiritual connection, simply to compensate for my loss—was this a type of desperation related to deep, unresolved grieving, or was I having authentic experiences? Was my intuition correct and somehow these orbs were related to the human soul or consciousness? If they were real, were they giving me another clue about the survival of consciousness?

CHAPTER SIX

*"Find a place inside where there is joy
and the joy will burn out the pain."*
~ Joseph Campbell

Embrace the Gift

The more I tuned into my inner guidance and connected to God, Source and I AM Presence, the greater my desire to listen and look for Spirit. It was as if my son's death had turned on my spiritual awareness. The messages were everywhere; I just needed to pay attention. This tenuous thread was a lifeline that often rescued me from the sadness and grief.

As I began to keep a journal of these experiences, they reminded me that I was not separate from Spirit or my son, but a part of both. These precious moments carried me through those times when I thought I could no longer carry myself. They came in different ways and at different times. I realized I was not to judge the process, but to embrace each experience as a precious gift from God.

Whenever I stood steadfast in my intuitive *knowing* that we live on after-death, it seemed I was rewarded by contact with my son and Spirit. I experienced hundreds of after-death communications. I felt Chris's touch and presence, had visions and vivid dreams, experienced electrical phenomena, unusual animal encounters and synchronistic events; and heard a voice that saved me from serious injury. The validation from those precious moments gave me relief from the physical and emotional pain of grief.

With each spiritual experience, another tiny piece of me healed. With great anticipation, I looked forward to these connections with my son.

Valentine's Day

As the five-year anniversary of my son's death approached, I realized that friends, family and I had had so many after-death communication experiences with Chris that I decided to write a book about them. I wanted the people who were closest to me to read the wonderful stories as a reminder of the miracle of Spirit in our lives.

There was no hurry or deadline. My intention wasn't to heal myself per se, but to share my story with others, hoping it might ease their pain if they had experienced similar losses.

In January 2011, I spent two weeks working on the manuscript, feeling excited and motivated. Then suddenly I fell into a deep depression. I had never felt like this before. Through my writing, I was reliving Chris's accident. I missed my son and writing about him made our physical separation all too real. As I continued to write down the moving experiences of contact with Spirit, I fell deeper into a place I had yet to venture. It was the hole of despair, which was always to my left, just inches from a misstep.

At a certain point, I stopped writing and moped around in my pajamas, not leaving the house for days at a time. I didn't tell my family how I felt, although my youngest daughter Olivia noticed. The pain was overwhelming and debilitating. I just didn't want to be here anymore. It hurt too much.

The sadness was so deep and profound. I missed seeing my son in person. I'd had five years to watch the aftermath of his devastating accident unfold in front of me. If I could get my daughter Olivia to stop by the grocery store or a fast food restaurant on her way home from school, she would at least have something to eat for dinner.

Honestly, I wasn't up to preparing a meal for her, although without fail, every day of her life I have made her school lunch and continued to do so during this time. I always felt it was important to say goodbye to her as she left for school each day. It was a dark time for me and I stopped taking orb photos. This confirmation of their presence had always filled me with joy. In fact, Olivia would often tease me, saying that I loved the orbs more than I loved her.

That's not true, of course, but they are infinitely entertaining to watch as they zoom around the room illuminated by the infrared light on my camera. I usually laugh and tease them, and in return, they've given me some beautiful pictures. This time, however, even the orbs weren't able to lift my spirits.

As I sat moping on the couch watching TV, the lamp over the bar started to flicker. I knew Spirit was trying to get my attention, but I ignored the sign. It just didn't matter. My son was gone and he was never coming back. The flickering continued off and on for a while until finally I said aloud, "Okay already, I'll take the darn pictures!" Half-heartedly, I took several photos and tossed the camera back on the coffee table. Usually I reviewed my pictures. This time I didn't bother.

Several days later, when I finally recovered from my waning interest in the orbs, I scrolled back through the photos and noticed a beautiful pink orb by my angel in the living room, just a few feet away from the flickering lamp over the bar. It was date stamped February 14, Valentine's Day. (Photo 4) Please see OrbWhisperer.com for the colored photos.

The orb near the angel was significant to me because I always see her as the Angel of Love and Protection for my house. She brings peace and tranquility to my surroundings. When I think of her, I think of my son in Heaven.

It was difficult having these experiences and sharing them with friends and family when no one else, except for my girls, seemed excited about them. My only guidance and support were the few published books on orbs.

Klaus Heinemann, Ph.D., co-author of *Orbs: Their Mission & Message of Hope* states, "It is our position, then, that orbs appear in meaningful places in photographs, and not haphazardly; it is because they are there by design."[30]

Photo 4 (left) Valentine's Day Orb 2011. Photo 5 (right) Blue orb captured with same angel on June 16, 2011 © Virginia Hummel. Colored photos can be seen at OrbWhisperer.com.

The pink orb had appeared for a reason. My intuition told me that Chris was connected to it. Intuitively I knew he felt my sorrow and wanted to send me some love. It was his way of saying, "Mom, get up off the couch, stop moping, and find the joy that you feel when you take orb photos."

He was right. It was just what I needed to lift my spirits. I felt closer to my son and connected to God when I felt joy. Joseph Campbell said, "Find a place inside where there's joy and the joy will burn out the pain."[31] I never realized the wisdom of those well-chosen words until I discovered that my joy regarding the orb phenomenon helped me transmute the pain of my grief.

The appearance of the pink orb was not a coincidence; instead, I believe it was connected with my son. This was a significant experience for me in my grief journey and I wondered if anyone else was experiencing this kind of connection with orbs.

My friend Nancy Myers has also embraced the orb phenomenon and discovered the healing power of their presence. She has taken some wonderful photos of orbs in meaningful places.

Nancy – Visiting Orbs

It was through my website and the orb phenomenon that we met. While visiting Nancy in the fall of 2012, she suddenly stated she could feel both of our boys present. Grabbing her camera, she directed her husband Rob and me toward the back of the room. I laughed and told the boys to jump into the shot.

Photo 6 (left) Virginia Hummel and Rob Myers after requesting our sons to appear. Photo 7 (right) Orb appears after requesting an orb photo Christmas card. © Nancy Myers.

In Photo 6 appear two large orbs, one above Rob and me, along with several smaller ones. Is it a coincidence to find two "dust" spots positioned just above our heads in a meaningful place in the photo?

According to Klaus Heinemann, Ph.D., co-author of *The Orb Project*, "Airborne particles should always be in statistically random locations; the orbs would then have to be expected to show up in photos in statistically random locations—almost *never* in 'meaningful' locations."[32]

During the Holiday season of 2012, Nancy Myers grabbed her camera and stepped outside to her front yard. She had just asked Spirit for an orb photo for her Christmas card when she snapped this shot. (Photo 7)

It still makes me smile to see it. Is it Santa or better yet her son, Robbie, with a sense of humor? We may never know the real answer, but regardless of the identity of this soul, this photo stimulates our imagination and offers us the opportunity to make that leap of faith to reach out and connect with Spirit.

Were Nancy and I the only two who were experiencing orbs in meaningful places, or were they also appearing to others who had lost family or friends?

Debra

Debra Tuohy was a Facebook friend who always posted the most inspirational quotes and pictures while grieving her daughter, Shayna. I looked forward to opening my Facebook page each morning and reading her uplifting posts. She passed away less than ayear after her daughter crossed. Her sister captured an orb near a memorial spot in their garden just after Shayna's funeral. (Photo 8) Along with the bright orb, notice the heart shape on the tree that happened to appear just after Shayna's death.

Patricia

My good friend Patricia Alexander, award-winning co-author of *The Book of Comforts: Simple, Powerful Ways to Comfort Your Spirit, Body and Soul*, lost her beloved husband and soul mate, Michael Burgos, in August of 2011.[33] The following month I introduced her to the world of orbs, when I met her for the first time at a writers' Conference.

Since then, she has faithfully photographed an orb in her bedroom as she calls out to Michael to say goodnight. Patricia says that during this time of grief and adjustment, her connection with Michael through the presence of an orb has given her a sense of solace unlike any other.

On a trip to present her first keynote address after Michael's death, Patricia took a few pictures in her hotel room. She took seven pictures and was surprised that none of them contained orbs. She had fully expected Michael to be there with her on the eve of her first speech since his passing.

Photo 8 (left) © Debra Tuohy. An orb appears at a memorial site. Photo 9 (right) © Patricia Alexander. An orb appears when a deceased husband is requested to sit on a suitcase.

Undaunted, she called out to Michael and said, "I'm not going to stop taking orb pictures until you go over there right now and sit on my suitcase."

Photo 9 is what she captured after calling out to her husband. Michael had a sense of humor in life and apparently also in death. In the three years since her husband's transition, Patricia has been deeply focused on orbs. Above all, she remains open to the miracles possible through a connection with Spirit.

Carol – More Validation

Carol Danforth, R.N., shares a story in which she specifically asked a particular individual to appear as an orb. Carol says:

> On a very slow Sunday afternoon on the neonatal intensive care unit floor of the hospital, I let my thoughts drift to Dr. Mike, a much-loved pediatrician who worked with the

children and nurses on my floor. He had taken his own life a year earlier while suffering from end stage cancer. He loved children. I wondered if he was still present on the ward and would appear for me as an orb.

I pulled out my camera and stood in the hallway facing a small waiting area. "Dr. Mike," I said, "If you're here, I want you to sit in the middle chair." I was delighted to see an orb hovering above the middle chair. (Photo 10) I hurried to the other nurses and showed them the photo. All of them except one were amazed.

Photo 10 (left) An orb appears in the center seat after requesting deceased Dr. Mike to sit there. Photo 11 (right) An orb appears after requesting Dr. Mike to sit on left shoulder. © Carol Danforth.

"I don't believe it," said the skeptical nurse.

"It's true. I asked Dr. Mike to sit in the middle chair. It's him." I pointed to the orb again.

The skeptical nurse sat at her desk. "I don't believe it. Dr. Mike, if you're here, you sit your butt on my left shoulder right now." (Photo 11)

Carol snapped the picture. What are the odds that a single dust spot would happen to appear on the nurse's shoulder, positioned in a meaningful place in the photo? More and more people are discovering how easy it is to interact with spirit through orb photography.

Aunt Susan "Mimi"

My Aunt Susan passed away from cancer on March 15, 2015. It was the first time since my son's death that a family member I felt close to passed away. Susan was a terrific hostess, wife and the mother of five children and nine grandchildren. A week later, her family gathered with ours at an intimate memorial dinner we gave for them to honor their mother.

Her family knew that I took orb pictures but I don't think they ever really paid much attention to my work. Through my orb photography, I realized that I could give them an opportunity to experience firsthand this miraculous phenomenon and a connection to their mother in the afterlife.

The following photos surprised even me at how easily our family on the other side wants to communicate with us. Coincidently, my Aunt Carol also had cancer and crossed over the day of the party. My cousin, Virginia Dirschl, shared a favorite poem of her mother's during the memorial dinner when I captured an orb photo. After seeing the photo, many of her family agreed that the orb had to have been Susan. (Photo 12).

That evening as my cousin Kirk stood to remember his mother, I captured this photo. For me and the others at the party who saw the photo, it was obvious to all of us that both Aunt Susan and Aunt Carol were there with us. (Photo 13) I noticed that these photos gave them something to focus on other than their loss. They created curiosity and excitement along with the possibility that there really was something beyond death.

When I found Lillie, my Aunt Susan's wonderful caregiver who was by her side for over a year and the moment Susan crossed, and my sister-in-law, Katie, sitting together just after our large family dinner I said, "Let me see if I can take a picture of you both with Aunt Susan." I called out to Susan to join them. (Photo 14)

Photo 12 (left) An orb with Virginia Dirschl (standing) as she recites a favorite poem of her mother's. Photo 13 (right) Kirk Pereira, with two bright orbs during a memorial dinner for his mother. © Virginia Hummel.

Photo 14 (left) An orb appears after requesting that my Aunt Susan to join in the photo. Photo 15 (right) Caroline Pereira asked for "Mimi" to appear as an orb at her left shoulder. © Virginia Hummel.

My Aunt Susan's daughter-in-law, Caroline, asked me if I would be able to take a photo of her with "Mimi" as an orb. When I showed her the picture I captured she got excited and said that she hadn't said anything but that she had secretly asked for "Mimi" to appear as an orb at her shoulder. (Photo 15)

I witnessed how my Aunt Susan's family felt when I showed them the photos at the party. They were excited and joyful at a time when loss can weigh so heavy on our hearts. Even my staunchly skeptical Uncle Bill began to lean a little closer to embracing the orb phenomenon as a connection to our loved ones.

Barbara

I met Barbara Stone Bakstad at a spiritual conference. We had just come from James Van Praagh's session where my son came through in a reading. When that session ended, Barbara and I walked together into John Holland's session. He is a renowned psychic medium like James Van Praagh.

Barb had recently lost her son David and had hoped to hear from him through James. As we sat down in John's session and waited for it to begin, I began to pray silently for her to have a reading with David. I knew how healing it could be and felt she really needed it.

Barb received the second reading of the session from John. He pointed to the area where we were sitting and said, "I have a little boy here who drowned." Barb's sister stood up and said, "Yes, that's Adam. He was two and a half years old. He's my sister's son."

Photo 16 © Virginia Hummel. John Holland the moment he says, "I have your two boys here with me." (See arrows)

There was a collective gasp in the auditorium as our hearts went out to Adam and his mother. John proceeded to talk with Barb and then said, "I have a second male energy here who also drowned. Do you know who I am talking about?" The person John referred to was Barb's twenty-one-year-old son David who had recently died. After a short discussion with Barbara, John said, "I have your two boys with me on stage." I snapped Photo 16 at that very moment. Notice the two orbs with John to his left.

John tends to use humor as a wonderful way to shift the energy in the room as the circumstances surrounding the death of a loved one during a reading can be very emotional. John suddenly said, "There's a parrot sitting on my shoulder. Do you know anything about this?"

Barb blurted out, "The parrot drowned too!"

The audience laughed at the irony of the situation if only as a relief from tragic circumstances Barbara experienced. A storm had blown its cage over and the parrot escaped, only to be swept into the water.

Over the last few years as I have gotten to know Barb, I have discovered her wonderful sense of humor. Despite her losses, she uses it to help her find balance in her grief journey. We all needed some levity after learning she had lost two boys and we were grateful she was to be able to make a joke of the poor parrot's demise to lighten the energy in the room.

The part of me that is still skeptical these kinds of photos are possible must concede that the coincidence, position, and timing of these orb photos, especially in light of the fact these photos were requested of our loved ones and spirit, are compelling.

These photos and stories validated the experiences I was having with orbs. The idea that the orbs were connected to our loved ones was beginning to make sense and I wasn't the only one who thought so. Yet many of the people with whom I shared my experiences were skeptical. Part of me still shared that skepticism, even though I had seen an orb without the aid of a camera, continued to hear stories and see orb photographs of communications between humans and orbs. Were orbs really connected to the human soul?

Chris

On October 27, 2011, I captured orb Photo 17 in my kitchen. The face of a young child appeared inside it but I didn't further pursue the identity. Over the years, I would come across the photo and wonder whose little boy it might be. In September 2016, I came across a picture of my son Christopher at six years old and immediately saw the uncanny resemblance to the young boy inside the orb photo.

I enlarged and color contrasted the photo to discover the young child in the orb was my son Christopher. Imagine my surprise and delight to discover this after all these years. You can see the "v" part of his bangs above and to the right nose in both pictures.

Photo 17. (left) Cropped orb photo with face. Photo 18 (lower right) Enlargement of photo 17. Photo 19 (upper right) Christopher at six years old. © Virginia Hummel

As for these photographs, I find the timing and appearance of these orbs more than coincidental. Could the balls of light seen in digital photos, and sometimes by the human eye, be visual proof of life after death? Are we experiencing the presence of consciousness outside our bodies as an orb?

The beauty and truth of these stories and photographs give us the opportunity to make the leap and "get it" while we are here in this lifetime. Imagine how much comfort we all might have if we knew without a doubt, that death was just a momentary transition. Then, through this we discovered our loved ones live on.

These deeply moving examples from Spirit through orb and other spiritual encounters continue to grow in number around the world. We must ask ourselves how much more proof we need before we step from our willful ignorance, and acknowledge that consciousness and life continues after the moment of metamorphosis we call death.

Each of us has the opportunity to choose our "aha" moment. Those who have chosen to step into the light and embrace the idea that consciousness survives death are discovering they are not only experiencing life on multi-dimensional levels; they are also experiencing the miracle of connection to their loved ones who have transitioned before them. This extraordinary connection aids in our grief healing.

As I continued to photograph orbs, my excitement and joy would immediately encourage more of them to appear. Whenever I summoned orbs to appear, either by thinking about them or by verbally asking them to show up, they did. It was almost as if I had radar or some type of antenna that sent out a signal and they responded. The orbs were exhibiting a consciousness. Stunned by this discovery, I knew I needed definitive answers when I began to talk to them and they reacted.

How was this possible? Did I possess some magical ability to interact with Spirit, or had I tapped into a God-given ability innate in each of us?

CHAPTER SEVEN

"The light of the body is in the eye therefore thy eye be single, thy whole body shall be full of light."
~ Matthew 6:22

DMT: The Spirit Molecule (N, N-Dimethyltryptamine)

You may have heard stories about people who have had a miraculous experience with Spirit, visions of the Virgin Mary, an angel that arrives in time to save a life, the deep, rich and hyper-real experiences of a near-death occurrence, or visions, voices and signs of deceased loved ones.

Why does this happen to some people and not to others? Are they special, or is something else at work that creates the opportunity for these experiences?

As I started to seek answers to these questions, one particular explanation jumped off the page. Perhaps the communication or response is facilitated by DMT, a chemical produced by the pineal gland, a small pinecone shaped gland located in the center of the brain between the left and right hemispheres.[34] This location coincidentally aligns with the Hindu concept of the third eye, a spot above and between the eyebrows.[35]

The third eye is a mystical concept that relates to higher consciousness, insight and enlightenment. It is also associated with precognition, clairvoyance and out of body experiences (OBE). The third eye is sometimes referred to as the mind's eye.[36]

The pineal gland is also in alignment with the crown chakra at the top of the head.[37] The term "chakra," which is derived from the traditional Hindu system of medicine, refers to a spinning vortex of colored energy located in one of the seven spiritual centers of the human body.[38] René Descartes, a French philosopher, identified the pineal gland as the "seat of the soul."[39] Plato referred to this gland as the eye of wisdom.[40]

Photo 20 © Marlon Brammer. An orb appears at the third eye of a Buddhist monk.

DMT is found throughout nature and occurs in trace amounts in humans and mammals. For centuries, indigenous cultures, including Amazon natives, South American Shamans and American Indians have consumed ayahuasca and peyote (a plant based DMT) to achieve altered states, healing, and to connect with the Divine.[41]

During the early nineties, Dr. Rick Strassman conducted clinical research at the University of New Mexico by injecting volunteers with DMT or N, N-Dimethyltryptamine. He has written a book on the subject titled, *DMT: The Spirit Molecule,* which, according to the publisher, "makes the bold case that DMT, naturally released by the pineal gland, facilitates the soul's movement in and out of the body and is an integral part of the birth and death experiences, as well as the highest states of meditation."[42]

Although Dr. Strassman injected his volunteers with DMT, which created spiritual experiences, millions of other people have had similar experiences naturally. Meditation is known to produce effects similar to DMT, i.e. the ability to access different types of spiritual experiences. It is believed that the utterance of sacred words, chanting, breathing and sound or visualization techniques used in mediation can alter brain wave function, raising the vibration of the pineal gland and stimulating the release of DMT.[43]

Listening to audio or audio-visual recordings has also been known to passively produce transpersonal experiences that deal with states or areas of consciousness beyond the limits of personal identity.[44]

If DMT is the foundation for spiritually transformative experiences (STEs), could it also have been a catalyst for my ability to experience an almost daily connection with Spirit, and on occasion physically see orbs after my son crossed? Strassman's research shows that stress affects the release of DMT. Because the pineal gland is separate from the brain and protected by the blood-brain barrier, the pineal is not affected by adrenaline released by the adrenal glands: the fight or flight mechanism. Instead, the pineal gland is affected by the surge of adrenaline and non-adrenaline released by the pineal nerve endings.[45]

Could the extraordinary stress of my grief have altered my ability to secrete more DMT at specific times? During my early stages of grief, I felt as if I were physically vibrating. The more I thought about Spirit and contact with my son, the more joyful and euphoric I felt. The more joy I felt, the stronger the vibration in my body. Regarding the volunteers in his DMT research project, Strassman reports that "nearly everyone remarked on the 'vibrations' brought on by DMT, the sense of powerful energy pulsing through them at a very rapid and high frequency."[46]

At times, I am able to recreate this state and recognize the same incredible feeling of vibration. This is when I also experience increased ability to manifest the things upon which I focus. In Chapter One, "A Second Awakening," I describe this feeling as "swimming in champagne" or "getting ready to be shot out into the Universe." This experience can be also compared to the visceral feeling one receives from the vibration of a jet plane during takeoff, as the throttle pushes toward maximum thrust.

Kuan Yin

During the first few weeks following the death of my son, I experienced almost daily contact with Spirit. It was also a time when I felt as if I were constantly swimming in champagne. An incident that was particularly interesting occurred one evening less than two weeks after his accident. That morning I had an unusual experience with flickering lights in my house and knew without a doubt that it was Christopher. I could feel how these events energized and affected the vibration in my body, which seemed to increase my spiritual experiences and ease my grief. The following is an excerpt from my book, *Miracle Messenger*.[47]

> That evening, my eleven-year-old daughter Olivia came to me too frightened to sleep in her own room. The story of [contact with my son through] the flickering lights that morning had unsettled her, so I allowed her to crawl into bed next to me. In my nightstand drawer, I had placed the small book of spiritual prayers that I'd given to Chris years earlier. I found it in his own nightstand the weekend of his death when we cleaned out his room.
>
> I cradled the worn dog-eared pages against my heart for a moment as if somehow they would help me gain a small connection to him. Then I read aloud for twenty minutes, sometimes repeating the same verse over and over, more for my own well-being than for my daughter's, I suppose.
>
> Even though my first thought as a mother was to comfort and calm my little girl, I soon found myself melding with the

words. They came alive on the page, their meaning tangible as they rolled off my tongue until my daughter drifted off to sleep and my lids grew weary. I fell asleep remembering the excitement of the lights in the laundry room that morning and the anticipation of another contact with my son.

In the middle of the night, I awoke abruptly. Someone was in my room. Terrified, I lay on my right side with both hands tucked beneath my cheek and peered from the blankets that partially covered my head. I tried to move but was paralyzed. My heart pounded as adrenaline shot through my body.

Olivia lay next to me, still asleep. I couldn't even turn my head to see who might be standing next to her, much less try to save our lives. I lay motionless and listened intently for sounds of the intruder. My mind raced with what to do next.

As I stared past my nightstand to the narrow wall at the entrance to my bathroom, I noticed a small gathering of glittering white lights. I blinked to focus on what I was seeing. Was I awake or dreaming? I pinched my palm. I was awake.

The glittering white lights danced on my wall in an area the size of a dinner plate. They reminded me of strong sunlight on rippling water, although I didn't need to squint from their brightness to see them. (See Photo 21) I held my breath as they performed their shimmering dance and watched as they shifted from silver to gold. It was like watching the dazzling gold glitters from Fourth of July fireworks.

As I lay quietly watching the glittering gold lights, I forgot about a possible intruder. Then the lights turned from gold to sparkling translucent red chips about the size of a deck of cards. The lights encompassed the entire 4 x 9 foot wall.

Photo 21 © Virginia Hummel. An orb similar to the glittering white lights.

Mesmerized by the sheer wonder of it, there was no reflection from these lights anywhere else in the bedroom. My mind raced for an explanation. The most rational one I could come up with was that a police car with its flashing red light was in my back yard. The red light must be filtering through my blackout drapes and reflecting on the wall in front of me.

The moment I realized that scenario was impossible, fear shot through me once again. I knew that what I was witnessing was not of this Earth.

Never at any time did I feel afraid of the lights, but what I felt instead was fear of the unknown. As spiritual as I thought I was, nothing had prepared me for my reaction. It was too much for me to process.

In the next instant, the sparkling red lights vanished. I lay motionless for several minutes, attempting to recall every detail of the experience. I reached out for Olivia, breathing peacefully, and then lay awake for hours peeking out from beneath my covers. I was frightened, curious, and determined as I examined every scenario I could imagine, desperate for an explanation of what I had seen.

Ultimately, I could find none other than the reality that Spirit had visited me. It was one of the many profound events in my life. For the time being, I concluded that the lights were my son in Spirit.

The next day I was so excited and couldn't wait to tell everyone about the lights. Some loved the story and were really excited. This small group of friends and family who had had such experiences themselves were open to such possibilities. Others, of course, thought I was nuts.

For the next six months, I firmly believed it had been my son's presence in my room that night. I clung to that belief until I came upon a book by Doreen Virtue, Ph.D., titled *Archangels and Ascended Masters*.[48] Casually, I flipped through the pages and stopped when I came to a section about the Eastern Goddess named Kuan Yin. I began to read. I had no idea who Kuan Yin was and had never heard of her before now:

She is one of the most beloved and popular Goddesses of compassion and protection, and her name means "She who hears prayers." You may see the color red when she's around, such as red sparkles of light or a red mist that appears out of nowhere.[49]

Could it have been Kuan Yin who visited me with her sparkling red lights after I had delivered my heartfelt prayers? It had been twelve days since Chris had crossed over.

As a mother, I was still in a state of disbelief and shock. Waves of sadness washed over me as I contemplated never seeing or touching his physical form again. I allowed those moments of grief to rise, crest and recede, sometimes rushing them along because the thought of another moment of contact with my son brought relief and joy.

My whole body tingled for months as I seemed to be half caught between worlds. It was that "walking on air" feeling that nothing can touch you and everything else before that time seemed dull and void of life. I was floating somewhere above our human earthly existence, but not quite in the other one.[50]

As I look back, it was quite possible that I was in an altered state created by my highly sensitized physical and emotional condition, similar to what Dr. Strassman's volunteers experienced when injected with DMT.

Was this altered state a direct result of DMT? As humans, are we able to control the release of DMT, either consciously or unconsciously, as a God-given mechanism guaranteed to facilitate a connection to levels of consciousness outside of our own?

CHAPTER EIGHT

"The orb acted as a kind of an interpreter between me and this extraordinary presence surrounding me."
~ Eben Alexander, M.D.

Survival of Consciousness

The scientific community has long clung to the reductionist theory that the brain creates consciousness, and if the brain dies, consciousness dies along with it.[51] Science has also held that near-death experiences, hallucinations, dreamlike states or so-called spiritual experiences are brain dependent. In spite of these traditional beliefs, however, a growing number of doctors and scientists are acknowledging that consciousness survives death.

Eben

In 2008, Dr. Eben Alexander suffered a near-death experience (NDE) caused by an extremely rare illness called *E. coli* bacterial meningitis. As he lay deep in coma and on a ventilator, his neo-cortex, the part of the brain that makes us human and creates thought, was rendered useless.

As a highly trained neurosurgeon who has operated on thousands of patients, Dr. Alexander would have previously been one of the first to explain that NDEs are "fantasies caused by the brain under extreme stress." *E. coli* bacterial meningitis is typically fatal. In Alexander's case, his illness was so severe his doctors believed that if he lived he would most likely spend the rest of his life in a "persistent vegetative state."[52] That he survived his illness and returned with his memory intact is hailed as a medical miracle.

Eben Alexander's number one *New York Times* bestselling book, *Proof of Heaven: A Neurosurgeon's Journey into the Afterlife*, details his journey into "the deepest realms of super-physical existence." He is escorted through his near-death experience by a beautiful angelic being: a girl with golden brown hair and sparkling blue eyes. She accompanies Alexander as they ride on the tip of a butterfly wing through a world that was "vibrant, ecstatic and stunning."[53]

At another point during his NDE, Dr. Alexander finds himself in a black womb-like void. It was filled with a brilliant light that emanated from an orb. The void was the presence of God whom Dr. Alexander refers to as "Om." He says, "The orb acted as a kind of an interpreter between me and this extraordinary presence surrounding me…the orb, who remained in some way connected to the Girl on the Butterfly Wing, who in fact was she, was guiding me through this process."[54]

Dr. Alexander says that after documenting his experience, he then sat down to research NDEs. He was dismayed to discover that most people encounter a family member or loved one during their near-death experience. As a neuroscientist, he questioned the validity of his experience because the only person he had encountered was a stranger. Shouldn't his father, who had recently passed, been present?

Alexander had been adopted as an infant. Four months after he had awakened from his coma, he received a photograph from his birth family. It was of his youngest sibling who had died ten-and-a-half years before Alexander's NDE. Her name was Betsy and someone whom Dr. Alexander had never met.

According to Alexander, the following day as he stared at her photo, the world of the Here and Now and the world of the Afterlife collided. "There was no mistaking her, no mistaking the loving smile, the confidant and infinitely comforting look, the sparkling blue eyes..." It was Betsy. She was the angelic being, the Girl on the Butterfly Wing. Betsy had accompanied him throughout his NDE and was the "orb" that acted as an interpreter in the void between Alexander and the presence of God.[55]

The neurosurgeon's NDE account confirmed what my five years of experience and research with orbs had shown me: not only does life continue after our physical death, but the consciousness of our loved ones can manifest as the appearance of a brilliant ball of light. I wept for ten minutes after reading this account.

My mind raced. If Betsy could manifest her consciousness as a brilliant ball of light, an orb—isn't it possible that Christopher may have appeared in the physical realm to visit me that night in 2007 in a similar form? If so, couldn't some of the orbs that are appearing in millions of photographs around the world be the manifestation of consciousness of other departed loved ones?

It was the connection and breakthrough I needed and validated my intuition that our soul or consciousness energy could manifest as a ball of light. I was excited about this revelation until I read further about DMT and learned that science and skeptics concluded that a DMT "dump" creates a near-death experience or brain-based hallucination. My heart sank. Suddenly, that little seed of doubt began to grow. How could I be sure that Alexander's NDE with Betsy was real and not a brain-based hallucination?

As I pondered this dilemma, it occurred to me that the problem with the reductionists' theory was the appearance of his birth sister, Betsy. Regardless of whether Dr. Alexander's consciousness remained intact and functioning inside or outside of his body, we do know that Betsy's consciousness had to have survived ten and a half years from her death in order to connect with her brother, who had never met her.

According to Dr. Alexander, his badly damaged neocortex precluded the regions of his brain associated with a DMT "dump" from generating the aural and visual experiences needed to support the theory of a brain dependent hallucination.

Near-death experiences occur when the body is under extreme stress of impending death. Dr. Strassman states: "Massive surges of stress hormones also mark the near-death experience...It may also be a time when the protective mechanisms of the pineal are flooded and otherwise inactive pathways to DMT production turned on."[56]

Was it possible that both Dr. Alexander and the skeptics were only partially correct in their assertions about DMT's role in his NDE. Science states that consciousness is brain-based and thus transpersonal experiences attributed to DMT must also be brain-based. Yet there is overwhelming evidence that consciousness exists outside the body and a growing number of doctors and scientists who support this conclusion, including Alexander. With this understanding, it is our responsibility to investigate other kinds of "fact-based science" that may also be incorrect including the role that DMT plays in our body.

Rick Strassman also says of his volunteers "there seemed to be a clearly identifiable sense of movement of consciousness away from the body, such as 'falling,' 'lifting up,' 'flying,' a feeling of weightlessness, or rapid movement."[57]

With that in mind, I wondered if DMT was present in Alexander and instead, acted as a booster to facilitate his experience that occurred outside his brain? According to Alexander he was in extreme pain prior to his coma. What if, in the early hours of Alexander's illness, stress caused by the extreme pain from the effects of the meningitis forced a DMT "dump?" This "dump" then acted as a catalyst for the soul and facilitated its departure from the human body much like a rocket booster launches a space shuttle into orbit.

It seems reasonable to conclude that the level of stress and pain I experienced after Chris crossed over was different from the extreme stress and pain endured by Alexander prior to his coma. Yet during my grief, I also experienced a connection with consciousness apart from my own. I knew my experiences were real. Were Dr. Alexander's also real? Is it possible that DMT facilitated Dr. Alexander's near-death experience; an event that occurred outside his brain?

Could DMT be God's way of insuring that the soul is reconnected with the Divine at the moment of impending physical death or other traumatic life events?

Harry

Were there other documented near-death experiences, similar to Dr. Alexander's, which also revealed unknown information that could be corroborated after the NDE?

Author Harry Hone suffered an NDE from cardiac arrest. He has documented his experience in his book, *The Light at the End of the Tunnel*.[58] Harry left his body in Newport Hospital and briefly watched the doctors working to revive him. He then traveled at high speed and was drawn into a dark tunnel where he could see at the end "the indescribable, effulgently pure white world of 'light.'"[59] He also realized that Harry Hone consists of a "tiny speck or spark of light" and the light had left its body or house."[60]

Something else also happened to Harry during his near-death experience. He received knowledge about his long lost sister's whereabouts by a voice on the other side, which told him of her exact location. Separated as children during WWII, Harry and his sister hadn't seen each other for thirty-four years. They reunited after Harry's NDE. She was living in a country that was halfway around the world from his current home.[61]

George

P.M.H. Atwater is a noted authority on near-death experience and its after-effects. She is the author of fourteen books, including *Beyond the Light: What Isn't Being Said About Near-death Experience: from Visions of Heaven to Glimpses of Hell,* which describes the remarkable NDE of George Rodonaia, Ph.D.[62] Rodonaia was an outspoken Soviet dissident and atheist who was murdered by the KGB. After being run over by a car three times and pronounced dead, his body lay inside a cooler in a morgue for three days, during which time he experienced a detailed near-death experience.

At one point during his NDE, he visited a newborn that cried continually. He communicated telepathically with the infant and learned of a broken hip that occurred during its birth. When doctors started to perform Rodonaia's autopsy, his consciousness returned to his body. He startled the medical examiners and they rushed him to surgery. Three days later, despite his severe injuries, he was able to tell them of the crying infant.

A subsequent examination of the infant revealed the broken hip, which not only validated Rodonaia's near-death experience, but also validated the survival of his consciousness *outside* of his physical body. He returned from his near-death experience a completely changed man and devoted the rest of his life to God, serving as a minister.

These two NDEs appear to corroborate Dr. Alexander's experience of the survival of consciousness outside of the physical body. The number of medically documented near-death experiences continues to grow. At this point, there are far too many on record for anyone to continue to believe that consciousness dies when the brain stops functioning.

The consciousness of both Harry Hone and George Rodonaia during their NDEs had to have remained intact and functioning outside their body, giving both men privileged information in the spiritual realm, which was later corroborated in the material world. Harry learned about the whereabouts of his long lost sister and George Rodonaia discovered the infant with the broken hip.

As a grieving mother, it was exactly the type of reassurance I needed in order to understand that my son's soul or consciousness continued to survive. This validated the ongoing contact I continued to have with him. Even today, nine years after my son's death, I am still able to experience different levels of consciousness, outside of and apart from my own.

Good Vibrations

It is believed that altering brain wave function and raising the vibration of the pineal gland stimulate the release of DMT. If this is true, does the amount of DMT released by the pineal gland have a direct correlation with the type of spiritual event that follows? Are higher consciousness experiences, insight, enlightenment, precognition, clairvoyance, out of body experiences (OBE) and NDEs dependent on the amount of DMT flooding our brains?

George Rodonaia was attacked by the KGB and pronounced dead. Harry Hone temporarily died of cardiac arrest. Dr. Eben Alexander was in a coma with no functioning neocortex, and I experienced the death of a child. Did each of us experience consciousness separate and apart from the body: the three men as they separated from their physical bodies and connected with the consciousness of other individuals, and I in my state of grief as I connected with the consciousness of my son?

Could my experience have fired up the booster rocket but their experiences hit the "go" button? During the pain and stress of my grief, I noticed that the intensity of my vibration or energy level was greatly increased. I had a single-minded desire to connect with Spirit. Could the combination of these two occurrences have resulted in my ability to hear my son, feel his touch and presence, see Spirit, and interact with animals in unusual ways? Did it give me the ability to see and interact with orbs and have a number of other ongoing transpersonal experiences?

After reading Dr. Strassman's research, I believe the vibration I felt in my body was similar to the vibration the doctor's volunteers experienced when injected with DMT. Is it possible that DMT was released as a result of the stress from my loss? And is it possible that

DMT had provided the environment or created the opportunity for one spiritual event after another?

I also considered the possibility that the vibration I experienced had "tuned me in" to a specific frequency that connected me to my son's consciousness. This would be similar to adjusting the dial on a radio to tune in the frequency band of a certain station. It may also explain why spiritual experiences with massive amounts of DMT, like those of Rodonaia, Hone and Dr. Alexander reached different, possibly higher frequencies on the spiritual spectrum.

When my vibration increased, I noticed that the appearance of orbs and my ability to see and feel their presence increased. In addition, I've noticed over the years that whenever I consciously raised my vibration through joy and excitement, my ability to connect with Spirit and consciousness outside my own existence increased. I could physically feel my heart leap and experience a surge of excitement at the thought of connecting with Spirit. I could then feel this heightened energy coursing through my body as I called out to Spirit either verbally or telepathically.

Was the appearance of orbs purely coincidental or a response to my vibration or frequency at the time? The number of instances in which this happened seemed far more than merely anecdotal. In my opinion, they were responding to both my telepathic and verbal call and appearing in order to be photographed.

If this were the case, then orbs possessed some form of consciousness and an ability to connect with my own. Was I generating a particular wave pattern, frequency or vibration in my brain that enabled me to communicate with consciousness outside my body?

Traditional Hindu customs identify a specific point of the human body responsible for spiritual experiences that coincidentally aligns with the location of the pineal gland. I mentioned earlier that Descartes identified the pineal gland as "the seat of the soul." Were they onto something that Western Science is just beginning to acknowledge?

Could the pineal gland have a dual role: acting as both a homing beacon and transmitter for the Divine? We all possess this tiny gland. Although millions of people around the world are photographing orbs, some are unsuccessful. I've noticed that many who have the ability to "call them in" are also open to the presence of Spirit and believe in the survival of consciousness.

Might these beliefs or, more importantly, the feelings these beliefs generate, have a direct effect on our pineal gland and our ability to connect with the Divine?

The pineal gland is part of our basic human equipment. Is it possible that DMT could be the Spirit Molecule, assuring our everlasting connection to God and our reconnection to the Divine at the moment of death or during stressful life events?

CHAPTER NINE

> "There are two ways of spreading the light:
> To be the candle or the mirror that reflects it."
> ~ Edith Wharton

Near-Death Experience and Orbs

Dr. Alexander is not the first person to see an orb or brilliant ball of light during a near-death experience. Many people who have shared their NDE stories describe encounters with guides and angels that have manifested from a ball of light. Some even describe their own consciousness or soul as a ball of light.

Raymond

Dr. Raymond Moody is the leading authority on the near-death experience. He is a bestselling author of twelve books on the subject, including *Life After Life: The Investigation of a Phenomenon—Survival of Bodily Death*, (with a foreword by the late Dr. Elisabeth Kübler-Ross, a world expert on death and dying), which has sold over 13 million copies worldwide.[63]

In his book, he investigates more than one hundred case studies of people who experience "clinical death" and were subsequently revived. According to his interviews with people who have had NDEs, Moody says, "Furthermore, despite its lack of perceptibility to people in physical bodies, all who have experienced it are in agreement that the spiritual body is nonetheless something, impossible to describe though it may be. It is agreed that the spiritual body has a form or shape (sometimes globular or an amorphous cloud, but also sometimes essentially the same shape as the physical body.")[64]

The following are excerpts from individual accounts of near-death experiences in *Life After Life*, which appear to be describing the characteristics of orbs:

> When my heart stopped beating…I felt like I was a round ball and almost maybe like I might have been a little sphere—like a BB—on the inside of this round ball…[65]

> I could feel something, some kind of a—like a capsule, or something, like a clear form. I couldn't really see it; it was like it was transparent, but not really. It was like I was just there—an energy, maybe, sort of like just a little ball of energy…[66]

> My being or myself or my spirit, or whatever you would like to label it—I could sort of feel it rise out of me, out through my head. And it wasn't anything that hurt, it was just sort of like lifting and it being above me…[My "being"] felt as if it had density to it, almost, but not a physical density-kind of like, I don't know, waves or something, I guess:

> Nothing really physical, almost as if it were charged, if you'd like to call it that. But it felt as if it had something to it…It was small, and it felt as if it were sort of circular, with no rigid outlines to it. You could liken it to a cloud… It almost seemed as if it were in its own encasement…[67]

Dr. Moody's case studies echo the description of the orbs we have seen in photographs, as does Dr. Tony Cicoria's experience. He also had a NDE after being electrocuted and became an orb.

Tony

During the 2012 National Conference for the International Association of Near-death Studies (IANDS), I had the opportunity to listen to keynote speaker, Dr. Tony Cicoria. Tony is an orthopedic surgeon and in 1994, at the age of forty-two, he was struck by lightning while standing next to a telephone booth during a storm. The strike knocked Tony to the ground, stopping his heart. He recalled seeing his own body surrounded by a bluish-white light. A woman standing near him, who happened to be an intensive care nurse, began CPR in a desperate attempt to save his life. But Tony had already left his body. He was dead.

With cool detachment, he watched the event unfold and then turned away to climb the stairs nearby. As he did so, he noticed that his legs began to disappear as he climbed. He said he felt himself became a "ball of bluish white light." The ball was approximately three feet in diameter and then began to shrink. He felt an enormous sense of peace and well-being. Suddenly, he found himself back in his body revived by the CPR. He felt pain and anger and cried out, "Please don't make me come back."

After his NDE, Tony began to have an insatiable desire to hear classical piano music. He was compelled to learn to play the piano and compose the piece of music he'd heard during his NDE that now played relentlessly in his head. He said if he didn't practice the piano every day the song played over and over in his head until he did.

During Tony's keynote speech, I took two photos of him. Photo 22 was taken at the exact moment he mentioned that the song plays over and over in his head. Notice the orb attached to Tony's head. If orbs are connected to the human soul or consciousness, it is possible that Tony has a guide who is encouraging him to compose this music?

The bluish orb in Photo 23(see OrbWhisperer.com) was taken just after Tony finished playing the composition he'd written after his NDE on the piano. He had returned to the stage during a standing ovation. Tony said, "It took a million volts of energy to get me to make that leap of faith."

Photo 22 (left) Orb appears on Dr. Cicoria 's head. Photo 23 (right) An orb appears above Tony Cicoria after playing a song he composed on the piano after his NDE. © Virginia Hummel.

Carter

Author and researcher P.M.H. Atwater shares the near-death experience of Carter Mills in *Beyond the Light*.[68] While at work, a massive load of compressed cardboard that Mills was loading slipped out of control, slamming him against a steel pole. During his NDE, Mills describes himself as a ball of light:

> Instantly Mills's whole life began to play out, starting at birth. He relived being a tiny spark of light traveling to Earth as soon as egg and sperm met and entering his mother's womb. In mere seconds, he had to choose hair color and eyes out of the genetic material available to him and any genes that might give him the body he would need.
>
> He bypassed the gene for club footedness, and then watched from a soul's perspective as cells subdivided. He could hear his parents whenever they spoke and feel their emotions, but any knowledge of his past lives dissolved.
>
> Jesus and the angels disintegrated into a giant sphere of light once Carter no longer needed their shape or form to put him at ease. As the sphere grew it absorbed him, infused him with the ecstasy of unconditional love…He zoomed back to his

mangled remains as a ball of all-knowing light and crashed into his solar plexus with such force it jolted his body to action.

Reece

Dr. Reece Manley, author of *Crossing Twice: Answers from the Source*, wrote that during his NDE he wanted to see God. What he witnessed was a huge, brilliant orb he came to know as Source. Dr. Eben Alexander, author of *Proof of Heaven*, also witnessed God as an orb. Reece also saw smaller orbs coming out of and returning to the large orb which he identified as Source. They were all connected to each other by what appeared to be beams of light.

Rachel

The following story is taken from Dr. Long's website NDERF.org (Near-Death Experience Research Foundation). After being hit by a car, Rachel describes "popping" out of her body and becoming a golden orb.

> I was hit by a car as a pedestrian. At the moment of being hit, it became surreal. I knew as the car hit my left leg that it was happening but everything began happening in slow motion. After hitting the windshield, I was thrown sixty-five feet and remember flying through the air. As I hit the pavement and started sliding, I felt I should leave my body.
>
> When my body came to a stop after sliding on the pavement, I "popped" out of the body and continued upward beyond my control but felt the body was "no good" and accepted that I was "moving on." After experiencing a period of time that I was in complete darkness and only felt myself being pulled through buoyant barriers, I came upon an opening. I then was greeted by five to ten golden "orbs" which I felt I knew and it was like a "reunion."
>
> It was the most joy and ecstasy I had ever felt when they greeted me. I knew them within. One orb approached me

and showed me that I was the same, and when it combined with me, I realized that I was also a golden orb. I was then pulled back and even more quickly than I had gotten to this other world, I was back in my body.⁶⁹

As a mother whose child has died in a motorcycle accident, my one hope was that Christopher didn't suffer. I had heard stories how we just pop out of our body at the time of death, but I didn't really know for sure if they were true. I saw the accident scene photos and the metal pole he impacted before landing in a ditch. As parents, we would do anything to protect our children, even take their pain if possible. But I wasn't there that night to protect him or hold him as he took his last breath. My mind can only imagine the pain and suffering my child must have felt on impact and the moments afterward.

Yet Rachel's story and many others like it have lifted a great weight off my shoulders knowing at the time of impact it was possible they just "popped" out of their physical body and continued living, consciousness and all. Not only were they still alive, albeit in a different form, they were loved and cared for by beings on the other side, many of which were friends and family who had also crossed over. If that was the case, then it was possible that my son also "popped" out of his body and was being loved and cared for on the other side too.

Corroborating an Orb Experience

While attending the August 2012 National IANDS Conference, I had the opportunity to listen to Dr. Alexander's keynote presentation, "Consciousness and the NDE: Beyond 2012." At one point, he seemed visibly moved as he spoke of "The Girl on the Butterfly Wing." I could feel his outpouring of heartfelt emotion the moment he realized it had been Betsy, his birth sister, who had accompanied him on his near-death journey.

Physically and intuitively, I could feel an energy or consciousness present in the room and I was compelled to reach for my camera. I *knew* his sister was here with him. I snapped one picture of the stage and screen the moment he revealed the photograph of his guardian angel, Betsy.

Betsy was glorious—radiant, as she stood in the warm glow of a California sunset with her golden-brown locks and the sparkle of divine light in her blue eyes. There were audible gasps from the audience as they recognized with clarity the truth behind this picture and the powerful message it held for all of us.

The photo on my camera flashed before my eyes, a brief, shining glimpse of the truth we all seek. There were several wispy orbs in Photo 24, but one especially bright orb next to the large photograph of his birth sister.

In all the years of photographing orbs, I have never attempted to identify the light beings in the photos. Although I can feel their energy, I prefer to allow the beholder of the photograph to use their own experience and intuition as a guide to the identity of the specific orbs they capture.

This particular photograph is an exception. Because I felt such a strong energy present in the room with us before and after Dr. Alexander revealed the identity of "The Girl on the Butterfly Wing," and because of the position of the bright orb, I intuitively knew the instant it flashed on my camera screen, that I had captured his beautiful sister in her full magnificence as a spark of divine light.

The moment was so powerful for me that it brought tears to my eyes. What are the odds that I would capture a brilliant ball of light next to "Betsy's" photo with one shot?

When the presentation ended, I stood just outside the lecture hall talking about the photo. Nola Davis, CEO of a health care corporation and tireless advocate for the education of seniors regarding the spiritual aspects of death, overheard my conversation and stepped forward. Nola is the co-author of *Live From the Other Side*, which combines the areas of spirituality, hospice, bereavement, personal growth and metaphysics.[70] She is also an intuitive.

NEAR-DEATH EXPERIENCE AND ORBS

Photo 24 © Virginia Hummel. An orb appears near the right side of the screen in the exact moment Alexander reveals his deceased sister as "the girl on the butterfly wing."

Nola said she watched a beautiful bluish-white light follow Dr. Alexander onto the stage and was surprised that it formed a full apparition of a lovely woman standing just behind his shoulder. She jotted down her description in a journal and noted that the woman was present during his lecture. As Dr. Alexander spoke from his heart, she moved closer to him on his right side. When he ventured into his scientific mode, she stepped away.

At one point, Nola said she looked up and second-guessed what she was seeing and experiencing as the woman stood behind Alexander. Suddenly the woman captured Nola's gaze and she heard her say telepathically, "You stick to what you know…" which meant to Nola that she was not to doubt what she was seeing or experiencing. Then Nola telepathically said, "Thank you for the gift."

Nola was stunned when Dr. Alexander revealed Betsy's photograph on the screen; it was the same woman she had seen standing behind him on the stage. Later, Dr. Alexander confirmed that he too felt his sister's presence with him during his lecture, as he had during past lectures on his near-death experience.

Nola's description of Betsy as a bluish-white light validated my photo of the bluish-white orb next to Betsy's picture. I don't believe it is a coincidence that Nola saw Betsy behind Alexander while I Betsy's presence and was urged to pick up my camera.

Claude Swanson, Ph.D., author of *Life Force, The Scientific Basis: Breakthrough Physics of Energy medicine, Healing, Chi and Quantum Consciousness* says, "Many phenomena are seen by 'sensitives' or clairvoyants, even though they do not appear on photographic film...most photographs taken reveal only a spot of light, an orb."[71]

It was intriguing to me that a physicist was able to embrace the idea that consciousness could exist outside the physical body when the majority of the scientific community believed otherwise.

"Are orbs are connected to the afterlife?" I asked during an interview for my grief documentary.

Swanson answered, "Nurses and hospice workers who are present at time of death have reported in many cases an orb leaving the body...In the out of body experience (OBE), the astral body, or sometimes the mental body is used as a vehicle. A self-contained subtle energy field, which we usually perceive as an orb, is created into which consciousness is placed, and can travel while the physical body remains behind.[72] ...This may explain why orbs are sometimes seen at death, and are considered to contain the consciousness after-death. This is the beginning of a scientific understanding of the "soul."[73]

David

I recently read Eben Alexander's new book, *The Map of Heaven: How Science, Religion, and Ordinary People Are Proving the Afterlife* and discovered the following story from David Palmer. It was so compelling that I immediately contacted David for an interview. He relayed the events of his father's passing:

> My father had been in hospice for nearly two weeks after suffering a series of strokes in August of 1999. Our family had finally made the difficult decision to let him go from his unresponsive state. My three siblings and I remained on a constant vigil in the hospital the last few days before he crossed, so that he was never alone.

At four o'clock AM, dad's breathing slowed and signaled the end was near. We sat in his darkened room, lit only by a small night-light attached to the wall near the bathroom. There was no equipment or monitors with lights in the room, which was located on the sixth or seventh floor of the hospital. There wasn't any other ambient light, not even from the window.

Seated in a chair a foot from his bedside, I stared at my father. He was facing me as he took his last breath. As I began to rise from my chair, I noticed what appeared to be a three-eighths inch to one half-inch piece of white thread or something similar that had settled on my dad's temple. I suddenly thought, *the nerve of that piece of thread to land right there! Where in the heck did it come from?*

I wanted to flick it away. I shouldn't have been able to see a tiny thread or piece of lint on my father's temple because of the darkened room. While I could see the outline of his eyes and hair, it was so dark that if I hadn't known him, I wouldn't have been able to distinguish the color of his skin.

Dumbfounded, I stared at the thread and wondered where it came from and why it appeared illuminated. I glanced up and searched the ceiling and room for another light source but found none. As I stared at the thread, it almost looked as if it were trying to stretch, similar to the movement of butterfly wing emerging from a cocoon. This little thread appeared to have movement in it, and for a second, I wondered if a bug had landed on my dad's head. Now, I'm almost mad and thinking, *Come on! He just died and something landed on his head!*

Suddenly, I noticed a little brightness coming from underneath the thread. At this point, I'm completely mesmerized, but I couldn't make sense of what I was seeing and rubbed my eyes to refocus. Tiny little rays of sparkling light begin to appear. As they grew, an iridescent sky-blue color appeared with the sparkling rays.

It may have been five or ten seconds later that a little blue orb slowly emerged from my dad's temple. Once free, it rested for a moment on dad's skin, balanced on the rays of sparkling light that acted like legs. Then it slowly rose a foot or two above his head, hovered for a few seconds, then purposefully moved off toward the southwest corner of the room. Oddly, it happened to be in the same direction as his childhood home located a block away. I turned to follow it and watched the little blue orb rise up and disappear into the ceiling.

Stunned, I turned back towards my siblings at the foot of his bed and stared at the silhouette of my younger sister, Jackie. I fully expected someone to say something, but no one did.

"Did something just happen here?" I asked, not wanting to put words in their mouths.

Jackie replied, "You mean that light that just came out of the side of dad's head and floated away?"

She had seen it too, but my older brother and sister who were standing behind my little sister at the time had not.

Jackie says, "I only saw very bright, sparkling, bluish-green lights dancing on the side of dad's head, twinkling. It makes me smile whenever I think of it. They seemed to stay there, dancing around by his temple. He was a very dear, funny man, very smart, and a bit sarcastic. I felt he was saying goodbye by twinkling at me—I was his baby and looked a lot like him.

David and his sister each received a wonderful gift that night, one in the form of an iridescent, sky-blue orb with sparkling rays and the other as bright sparkling bluish-green lights. Could the orb and sparkling lights that emerged from their father's head have been his soul or consciousness? The little sky-blue orb appeared to have acted with intention as it rested, rose, hovered and headed off in a specific direction after it emerged from his father's temple.

David's description of the thread that appeared on his father's temple reminded me of Alan's story where he describes "'something white' like *seeing a piece of fur from my ginger and white cat* but, as I took a step forward, the "something white" suddenly transformed into a spinning circle of light."

Is it possible that both of these experiences are describing the same thing? Could what David referred to as a thread that transformed into an orb, and what Alan referred to as a piece of fur which transformed into a circle of light be connected to the human soul?

Their experiences validated my research, experience and intuitive *knowing* that orbs are connected to the human soul or consciousness. Many near-death experiencers have described their "soul" as a ball of light or orb. They have also referred to others as a spark, orb, or being of light during their journey to the other side.

These descriptions seem to mimic the characteristics of orbs that we see in digital photography and help to validate my theory about orbs and their connection to the human soul. Could David's orb be the final piece of the puzzle needed to prove that consciousness survives death and is able to manifest as an orb?

CHAPTER TEN

"Ask and it is given to you; seek and you will find;
knock and the door shall be opened for you."
~ Matthew 7:7

The Urge to Know

Although countless near-death experiencers know for sure that there is life after death, many of us still wonder if there is something more. Imagine for a moment that death isn't an ending but a metamorphosis, a shedding of our physical body to reveal our authentic self, a shift to our natural state of being that is so comforting and real, once we have experienced it, we can no longer envision ourselves in any other form.

What if we could see this state of being? What if there was a way to see the other side of death, a manifestation of our authentic self, our soul, or consciousness energy? What an incredible thought! Imagine the implications of finally knowing without a doubt that we are more than just our physical body and that we really do live on after-death.

Imagine the comfort of realizing that our loved ones who have crossed before us are still safe and very much "alive." They have only made the shift from a physical to a spiritual state, like a caterpillar to a butterfly. Life doesn't end with our physical death, but continues on eternally in a different state of being. David Palmer's experience with the tiny orb emerging from his father's temple and the appearance of

Betsy as an orb during Dr. Alexander's NDE has given us beautifully documented examples of this. They both had a unique experience, and a profound awakening and healing through the miracle of Spirit.

Awakenings come in many forms, but are most commonly triggered by some sort of sudden emotional or physical trauma. Dr. Stanislav Grof, author of *The Adventure of Self Discovery: Dimensions of Consciousness and New Perspectives in Psychotherapy and Inner Exploration* writes:

> Experiences of encounters with guides, teachers, and protectors from the spiritual world belong to the most valuable and rewarding phenomena of the transpersonal domain…Sometimes they appear quite spontaneous at a certain state of the spiritual development of an individual; other times they suddenly emerge during an inner crisis, responding for an urgent call for help.[74]

In the book, *A Soul's Journey,* author Peter Richelieu also writes about how our urge to know more about life on the spiritual plane develops after a crisis. He writes:

> It required some great tragedy, such as the death of his well-loved brother Charles, to make him clamor for light, for occult knowledge; there had to be a crisis for through this, the urge to know is born.[75]

My own "urge to know" came in February 2006 when my youngest son Christopher died in a motorcycle accident. The loss of a child is one of the most painful and profound emotional experiences we can have. We question ourselves and our beliefs. We question almost everything about our life and we ask why. Why did it happen to us? What did we do wrong?

I'd heard that with tragedy came the opportunity for spiritual growth. I knew through reading and experience that I was the creator of my reality. Why wasn't I also the creator of my experience with death as well? I had the choice to create grace or despair. I chose grace because for me there was no other option.

How else could I make sense of all the harsh realities in the world: the wars and starvation, cruelty, utter inhumanity and indifference—even the loneliness, pain and heartache of my own experiences? There had to be a reason for all of this. Life had to have a greater purpose. Surely there was a larger picture. Otherwise, life seemed too inhumane. Why would anyone want to participate?

William Peters, MFT, M.Ed., is the founder of the *Shared Crossings Project*[76] in Santa Barbara, California. He suffered an NDE during a high-speed skiing accident at the age of seventeen. During our interview, William said:

> I remember being in the tube or tunnel and I realized I had been here before hundreds if not thousands of times. There was a real weightiness to that realization in a certain way because human lives have a purpose and a lot of them are quite painful. I have come to learn that being on Earth is like school.
>
> You check into a school with an intention and a set of objectives for a higher cause to evolve the soul. It wasn't just for my benefit or one soul, but for the benefit of all beings. These are work missions. It's not to say there's not joy in human life, there is, but the real intention, as I see it, is that we come with specific objectives.

The death of my son created a black hole too frightening to comprehend. The thought of his absence, his total obliteration was so overwhelming, the pain threatened to consume me. I knew I wasn't going to survive it unless I clung to the knowledge and belief I had possessed since childhood that there was indeed a bigger picture. I believe there has to be a reason and meaning to everything we experience as a human.

Therefore, I believe my son's death happened for a reason. With that in mind, I was determined to find that reason. The Carmelite nuns say my son was neither lost nor dead, but instead, "at a different address." If this were true, I just needed to find his address. Then I could communicate with him, and with his help, I would find some answers. In the process, I could not only help myself; I could also help others who were going through the same experience.

It was a hell of a challenge but I chose to stand in grace, to honor my son by being the best I could be, to have unwavering faith in my belief that life is eternal. I could have let this event destroy me, but instead I let it inspire me. I chose to grasp the opportunity to awaken and embrace the growth presented by this tragedy.

Louis LaGrand, Ph.D. is one of the world's leading grief counselors and author of several books including *Love Lives On: Learning from the Extraordinary Encounters of the Bereaved*. He says that the pivotal question all mourners face is: "Will I be loss oriented or restoration oriented? Will you make sorrow your way of life or will you choose a path to peace?"[77]

Attending Dr. LaGrand's workshop in 2011 was a privilege. He is kind, compassionate, funny and an exceedingly bright light who brilliantly shifts the dark energy of mourning the loss of a loved one into an event that were are able to manage and even overcome. It was a huge relief to know that he validated the way I chose to move forward and be restoration oriented after the loss of my son despite how others felt. Moving forward that way brought me peace.

It is interesting to note that the Universe is right on track, regardless of what I experience, or how difficult the challenge. My life has been one synchronistic event after another. By focusing the direction of my thoughts and aligning myself with God, Source and I AM Presence, I allow the grace of all that is, to flow through me.

It is my job to encourage that grace to unfold with abundance, joy and miracles. When I stop that flow through fear or negative thinking, my experiences follow that train of thought. It has taken a lifetime to understand the degree of power and responsibility involved in creating every moment of my life, whether those moments are joyous or painful.

This doesn't mean that I didn't grieve the death of my child. I curled into the fetal position and wailed with the best of them. Although my spirit knew with unerring certainty that my son was fine, my heart was broken. Despite my emotional and physical pain, I felt compelled to stand in the light, to look up, not back, to cling hard and fast to my intuitive *knowing* that we are more than just a physical body.

Almost immediately after Chris's departure, I started to receive signs that he hadn't left after all. I had taught my son about life after death and had always believed there was more to life than what we could physically see.

Dr. Alexander's experience of meeting his birth sister during his NDE strongly suggests that my instincts of life beyond this third dimension were correct. My memories and *knowing* at a young age were not just those of an active imagination; they were an actual recollection that there was indeed something much more to life than my physical existence in this dimension. It also meant there was a strong possibility that my son Christopher had survived in some other form.

Life as an Eternal Being

Many who experience near-death return with the overwhelming knowledge and feeling that *love is the key to everything*. We must consider that the real, unconditional love and acceptance NDErs speak of is the result of spiritual evolution or balance.

Over the course of my life, I have read many books that state we are eternal beings. As eternal souls, we make repeated journeys and may experience hundreds, if not thousands of lifetimes in physical form to achieve this balance. Before our birth, we choose the experiences that will best help us with our spiritual development. Thus, we undertake our earthly experiences with the ultimate goal of reaching this divine place of acceptance, love and non-judgment for one another, and ourselves despite the differing paths we may choose to arrive there.

Each of our journeys is different as is our carefully crafted exit plan designed in our pre-birth contract. These pre-birth contracts can be made with many different souls at the same time. Souls can volunteer to leave early in order to offer those left behind a learning opportunity. This can be both sad and painful. My son left behind his five-year-old son. It has been difficult to watch Logan grow up without his father. Despite this information, it may take a lifetime to understand and accept why our loved ones left when they did.

Through many lifetimes, these learning opportunities offer us a chance to find a place of balance by experiencing all sides of an issue to help learn unconditional love and non-judgment. I realized that if this were true, it meant that I was experiencing another side of an issue with the death of my son. Among other things, it was an opportunity to learn unconditional love and non-judgment along with compassion for others who have also suffered a loss.

Did I need to learn how to experience my son's death from a point of love and not anger? Was his death an opportunity to find a place of balance within a very deep and painful experience? Was it an opportunity to keep my faith in God that He in His infinite wisdom knows what is best for not only my soul growth, but also for Logan and Chris?

The answer is "yes" to all three of those questions. From the moment I learned of his passing, I realized my lesson was to view it from love and compassion for my son, myself, and those affected by his death. Somehow, I knew this was where I should be but I struggled with forgiving his friend who had left the party drunk after an argument. When my son couldn't get a hold of him after repeated phone calls, he went to look for him. Unfortunately, Christopher was drunk too. In his concern for his friend's wellbeing, Chris jumped on his motorcycle. While his friend spent the night in jail for a DUI, my son died when he mistook a dead-end road for the on-ramp to the freeway to return home.

Part of me wanted to blame his friend for Chris's death. My mind was filled with "if only." The other part of me knew there was a bigger picture, a divine plan. I realized that forgiving his friend and recognizing that he lost Chris too was an important step in my healing, but it took a conscious effort to do so.

There were learning opportunities and gifts in this tragedy for everyone. Nobody escaped unscathed. It also took a conscious effort to embrace the notion of a pre-birth contract and reach out for a connection to God and Spirit. When I viewed this tragedy from a higher perspective, love and forgiveness, it lessoned my pain and aided in my healing. It was challenging, but it felt right.

Scarlett

It also felt right for Scarlett Lewis whose six-year-old son was killed at Sandy Hook. The circumstances surrounding her son's death was tragic. Scarlett had every reason to carry the anger from this senseless act of violence for a lifetime. Yet at Jesse's funeral, she responded to those who asked how they could help. "If you really want to do something to help, then do something that will help all of us by turning an angry thought into a loving one…if you want to help please choose love."[78]

It seems implausible that the circumstances surrounding Jesse's death could elicit anything other than great pain and a lifetime of anger towards a young man who caused so much devastation. Yet despite her loss, Scarlett was able to see how much pain and anger Adam Lanza had to have been in to do what he did. She understands how important it is to teach our children compassion. Scarlett has chosen love. While she has worked hard to arrive at a place of acceptance, she has forgiven the man who killed her son. Scarlett says:

> Hating Adam will not bring Jesse back. It will only hurt me and generate more hatred and anger.[79] Although Jesse's

death could have destroyed me, hope, love, forgiveness, and faith had saved me.[80]

Scarlett has found a place of balance within a tragic experience. She has acted with courage and wisdom despite her painful loss. Chris's death offered me the opportunity to also find a place of balance. By stepping into a place of non-judgment and embracing my faith in God and spirit, I was lifted up during a time of deep grief.

Some may wonder did we really need the loss of a loved one to jump-start our connection to Spirit and ultimately find a place of balance? Apparently, I did and it worked. It also jump-started my urge to know what life was like at a deeper and more profound level.

Through my grief, I discovered that my loss gave me the opportunity to reconnect with God. It's not that I had distanced myself from Him; it's just that I had immersed myself in daily life and had taken Him for granted. From the moment I heard Chris had died, I knew my son was with God. *My son was Home.*

Erica McKenzie, co-author of *Dying to Fit In*, says that during her NDE, "God and I stood together with our backs towards Heaven and we looked out at the stars. I was very aware that Heaven was right behind me. I could feel it. I felt the most powerful love coming from Heaven. I can't even describe it in human words. It was so wonderful that I knew I was finally Home. I never wanted to be separated from that feeling and from God again."[81]

Hearing Erica say she knew she was finally home lifted something off my heart. It was validation of my intuition and *knowing* that my son was home too. More than anything, I wanted to know he was safe and loved.

Whether or not we are conscious of it, we search all our lives for this connection only to discover in the end that the road home lies not in front of us, but inside of us. As Jesus said, "The Kingdom of God is within you."

I had to go within to quiet myself long enough to listen to the call home. Home is where my authentic self resides. It is the divine spark and my essence as a spiritual being that connect me to God and ultimately to you, the reader.

Home was where I knew my son was on the morning my brother called to tell me of his accident. Home was where I longed to return. It was the place of ultimate comfort and love.

Golden Light of Love

I was reminded of this connection after my son's death with an experience I had one afternoon. The following is an excerpt from *Miracle Messenger*.

> A year or so after my son's death, I visited an Australian shaman who lived in my town. She was a tiny woman with extremely short hair and a twinkle in her eye. I had been to several of her classes and decided I would like to do a Soul Retrieval.
>
> The Soul Retrieval helps people gain insight into a problem and/or to locate the lost part of their souls. These parts can be missing due to physical or emotional trauma that occurs in this or other lifetimes. The Soul Retrieval helps to heal the individual.
>
> A shaman can capture the fragmented parts of us through his or her connection with spirit guides and teachers. My shaman knew nothing of my son or family, except that Chris had passed.
>
> Blindfolded, I lay on my back on bed in a quiet room. The shaman mentioned that the blindfold was for her benefit, to allow her to move freely around me without feeling self-conscious.
>
> She chanted, drummed, danced and put herself in a trance state to enable her to contact my guides and family and to see my past.

The moment she started chanting, I felt my physical body sink into the bed. My soul or spirit rose several inches above my physical form. It felt as if each cell in my body were vibrating. I relaxed as best as I could and allowed her to do her work.

I could hear voices, and at one point it felt and sounded like a giant bird with a huge wingspan had descended upon the room. I could hear and feel its presence all around me.

About a half hour later it was over and she began to tell me what she saw. It was fascinating. She described accurately both my mother and father's personalities and my relationship with them. She also passed on information that no one else knew but me.

At one point, she said my son came into the room, grasped my hand and gently kissed the back of it. He said to her, "You know, my mom always knows when I'm in the car with her." It's true. I do know when Chris is in the car with me.

While driving, I often get a strong sense of my son's presence followed immediately by hearing "You're Beautiful" by James Blunt on the radio. During those moments I always have the urge to lay my right arm, with my palm upwards, across the armrest. I never questioned those urges but just went with them. I knew every time this happened that Chris was sitting next to me holding my hand.

After we finished the session, it was time to pick up my daughter Olivia at the elementary school. As I was driving along, suddenly I felt my heart chakra[82] open wide and connect with divine love. I had a vision in my mind's eye of Jesus surrounded with a luminous aura of love and golden light. It was as if I had a direct link to Jesus and He offered the unconditional love that one feels in His presence.

> The only way I can describe it is to imagine a ten-inch round river of golden light brighter than the sun, starting at the center of my chest and connecting to His entire being. It was so filled with the most extraordinary love, tears of absolute joy and exaltation ran down my cheeks. For the next twenty minutes, I found myself in a state of grace feeling as if the highest form of Love was filling every part of me. I felt so warm and safe, cradled in this Love. Somehow, I managed to end up safely in the school parking lot. I surely don't remember most of the drive.
>
> During this event, I had an epiphany. I realized that all my life I had been seeking that specific love with a man, and none of these relationships had ended well. I also realized that no man on Earth is capable of that love. It was a divine love and the experience meant that I had unknowingly been searching for it all this time. I had *remembered* what it felt like to be in the presence of Christ and connected with unconditional divine love and my authentic self. I had memories of being on the other side.

Jeff

Jeff Olsen, near-death experiencer and author of *I Knew Their Hearts*, had a similar experience. He says:

> Knowing that such unconditional love existed beyond the veil left me feeling empty at times in this realm. I found myself searching for that same love I had experienced in my brief visit to the hereafter. The gaping hole in my heart yearned to be filled. Too often, I looked to external influences to fill the void inside of me. I expected my new wife to fill me up and make me whole...looking outward for wholeness was a losing and painful battle.[83]

While Jeff had revisited the other side during his NDE, I had not been to the other side this lifetime that I recall, yet our experiences were similar. We both longed to connect with the unconditional love from the other side and were unsuccessful in our attempt to find it from someone else. We discovered that turning inward was the answer to this dilemma.

Our Authentic Self

Finding my authentic self was a key to finding the road Home. The challenge we face lies in recognizing the difference between our personality self or ego, the small 's', or our authentic spiritual self, the large 'S'. The death of my son gave me the opportunity to experience this.

When we recognize ourselves as spiritual beings 'S', we can watch our lives unfold with compassionate neutrality. This includes learning to view the loss of a loved one as part of a greater plan, one that is always unfolding, where there is no separation. When we find that place of balance we are then able to step away from the pain and conflicts created through judgment by our human personality and self 's', and experience the overwhelming peace and joy available to us from our spiritual nature and perspective 'S'.

An example of this would be judging the death of my son as either "something done to him" or "something done to me." These thoughts are from self or 's' and place me squarely in the lower vibration of blame, anger and guilt. This point of view serves neither my family nor me. Instead, through my pain and grief, I choose to look for the lesson and the gift in the experience and view my experience from my authentic self or 'S'.

The duality of 's' and 'S' is an inner conflict inherent in the nature of man. The perspective from which we choose to operate will determine our response to the types of experiences presented to us. When I chose to view my son's death from 'S' instead of 's', I was rewarded by the miracle of God and Spirit through hundreds of after-death communications (ADC's). During a time of the deepest grief, I was greatly uplifted.

If we consciously choose to view life though 'S', then we have the ability to release any painful experience and replace it with an abundance of miracles and joy. When I found myself operating from 's' and feeling like a victim, forever separated from my son, I experienced a profound sense of helplessness, pain and guilt. I was trapped in a mire of misery.

Losing a child is one of the toughest lessons and I wondered why I'd picked that one as my call to action. How could that lesson possibly help me evolve spiritually? How could I arrive at and remain in a state of compassionate neutrality over the death of my son? Yet, how could I not achieve that state of compassionate neutrality when I take into consideration that I now know that I am a spiritual being having a human experience?

Losing a child seems like the ultimate challenge to put this theory to the test. In the book, *Your Soul's Gift: The Healing Power of the Life You Planned Before You Were Born,* author Robert Schwartz delves into exploring the pre-birth planning of spiritual awakening.[84] He tells of Pamela Kribbe who channels Jesus and who says, "That life challenges which are planned by your soul does not mean that you are doomed to experience all the fear and pain they might cause. You have free will. You can choose to overcome them. Instead of becoming suffocated by negative emotions, you can heal and transform your challenges. Ultimately, they are there to remind you of your greatness, not your smallness."[85]

For me, those words have never rung more true. Schwartz adds: "There is a space within you from which you respond. When you become aware of this space, you also become aware of who you really are: not a victim, but a powerful creator. From this awareness healing is born."[86]

This is the place I recognize as Source, higher consciousness, and our connection to God. I have come to realize that Chris's death was a gift. It was a catalyst, an opportunity to awaken to spirit, my authentic self 'S' and my full potential and power as an eternal being. It took a profound trauma to jump-start my urge to know, and what I discovered along the way only validated what I had known intuitively since childhood: *we don't die.*

Anita

In 2006, Anita Moorjani, comatose and hours from death, made a miraculous and complete recovery from end-stage Hodgkin's lymphoma. During her coma, Anita had a near-death experience (NDE) and was offered the option to return to life and be completely healed.

In her *New York Times* Best Selling Book, *Dying to Be Me: My Journey from Cancer, to Near Death, to True Healing,* Anita reveals that during her NDE she was told by some beautiful energy beings that upon her return lab results would show no sign of cancer.[87] Doctors were baffled by her quick recovery from the large tumors and open sores that riddled her body, but she was not. After her NDE, test results showed no sign of cancer.

While in her NDE, Anita experienced the overwhelming vastness of Spirit. She was shown that we are the creators of our "energy" or "vibration" and with that ability we allow sickness or health into our reality, along with everything else. "I saw all people as 'energy' and depending where our energy level was, that was the world we created for ourselves."[88] She said we all have the ability to heal ourselves.

Anita experienced a profound spiritual awakening during her NDE that today allows her to recognize the presence of Spirit in her daily life. Her most important message for us is to live our lives fearlessly.

> I no longer mourned for the deceased, because I knew that they'd transcended to another realm, and I knew that they were happy! It's not possible to be sad there. At the same time, I also knew their death was perfect, and everything would unfold in the way it was meant to in the greater tapestry.[89]

Without the loss of my son, I never would have had the incredible experiences with Spirit that confirms my lifelong *knowing* we are more than just our physical body. Through my son's death and my ensuing spiritual awakening, I am able to share my experiences with others so they too may find comfort knowing that life is eternal and death is just a moment of metamorphosis.

This is the message I chose to bring into this lifetime. Through his death, my son presented me with the opportunity to discover it. While it was difficult not to miss the human form that was my son, I also discovered it was possible to transform my grief, but it took my willingness to step outside the boundaries of the traditional grief experience to accomplish it.

CHAPTER ELEVEN

"Whether you think you can or you think you can't—you're right."
~ Henry Ford

Reframing Your Grief Experience

The grief journey is different for everyone. We have basic road maps, but no definitive way to grieve. Some of us can and do heal. For some, though, it can take a lifetime to find a place of acceptance for their loss. It is important that we honor our feelings of loss in whatever form they manifest. We miss the physical presence of our family member or friend and the void left by their death can seem overwhelming.

The important thing is not to set limits on our grief journey or our ability to heal. We *can* begin the healing process immediately. Yes, it is a process to find our balance, but when we lift our perceived limitations off the traditional grief experience, we can also lift our perceived limitations off our ability to heal. We realize anything is possible, even healing our grief.

Healing our grief is not forgetting our loved one or no longer experiencing moments of sadness. For me, there will always be an empty chair, especially as we gather during the holidays, yet I no longer choose to focus on the absence of my son, but on my newfound connection to him through Spirit instead. I have also chosen to embrace life and every precious moment I have left with the rest of my family. Healed grief means being able to talk about and honor our loved one in a proactive, positive way, and go on to participate in a life that includes joy and laughter. For many, it also means that we can continue to have a relationship with our loved one through the miracle of Spirit.

I sought grief counseling when Chris died. I needed someone on their own grief journey with whom to talk and share my experiences. While it helped to be with others who had lost a loved one, the atmosphere in the group was depressing. We each would take turns sharing our thoughts and feelings of how miserable and sad we were during the past week while the others sat quietly and listened. The moderator or group leader may have asked a question or two of an individual, but there was nothing uplifting in the experience. The vibration or energy in the room was very low.

While talking about our feelings was a start, where do we go from being sad, miserable and barely able to function? I wanted some immediate relief from my grief. I could tell the others needed it too.

Desperate to change the energy of the group, I began to regale them with the after-death communication with my son and the wonderful spiritual experiences I was having. I laughed, I cried, I was filled with joy and excitement as I shared these stories. At first, I received raised eyebrows that I dared to step out of the traditional mode of the group dynamics. I could tell the group leader was irritated. *This is not the way we do grief!*

But I persisted. As I did, I watched my experiences have a profound effect on the group. Slowly, as each week passed, someone else would share an experience and asked if I thought it might be their loved one trying to communicate with them. When I validated their experience, it lightened their grief. For a brief moment, there was joy and excitement in their eyes. It gave them hope. Suddenly, a completely new world opened up for them. There was light in the midst of a very dark time.

As a proactive individual, I am a doer and a fixer. Tell me it can't be done and I will find ten ways to do it. Yet, I felt utterly helpless and out of control from the death of my son. I wanted to jump in and fix it. I was his mother after all. On one hand, I honestly believed that I should have been able to prevent the accident, but there was nothing I could do to fix what had happened.

The only control I had was to make sense of what appeared to be a senseless loss. I needed a reason for the death of my son. I needed answers no one could give me. Instead of paralyzing me, it catalyzed me. It gave me a reason to get up each morning and search for answers.

Along with feeling a loss of control, it's common to also feel guilt, regret, blame or anger surrounding the conditions of our loved one's death. I desperately wished I had made different choices, fully convinced it would have affected the outcome. I berated myself for not being wise enough to see my mistakes ahead of time, or the strength and wisdom to have chosen differently. I struggled with guilt and regret until I used the shift in perception to help me move from our personality self or ego 's' and the lower vibration of guilt, anger, blame and regret, to the higher vibration of gratitude and our authentic spiritual self or large 'S'. This also brought me the opportunity to experience more contact with Spirit and my son.

Attitude of Gratitude

Gratitude is a vibration just like love, hate, joy or sorrow. When I felt gratitude for something during my grief, it shifted my energy or "vibration." It created a crack for the light to pour in. The more grateful I became, the more light poured in and I began to experience ADCs and contact with spirit and my son. I was in appreciation of these experiences and connections. I built upon the awe, wonder and joy I felt with each connection and in turn was blessed with even more daily miracles. Gratitude was the foundation that lifted me from grief.

Each day I would find something to be grateful for: my children, my grandson, a new bloom in my garden, a roof over my head. During the moments of deep despair, I looked for something in my tragedy that could make me feel grateful.

The top story in the news at the time of my son's death was the disappearance of Natalee Holloway, the beautiful high school senior who vanished in Aruba during her graduation trip. It was a parent's worst nightmare—the disappearance of a child. Our nation's heart and prayers went out to Natalee and her parents and we all prayed they would find her unharmed.

As a parent whose child had died, I couldn't begin to fathom the pain and anguish her parents must have felt not knowing where their child was or what had happened to her. And so in the moments when I felt sorry for myself, I would remember Natalee and her parents and think *at least I know where my child is.* It was a moment of clarity. Even in my darkest hour, I still found a reason to be grateful and it got me moving forward again on my healing journey.

One of the hardest things I had to learn as a parent was to let go and allow my child to explore the world and fulfill his mission this lifetime. I knew my son would die before I did. He knew it too. I could have spent every day trying to keep him from potential disaster, crazed and controlling, but I knew I needed to allow my son to live his life. I knew there was a divine plan, despite my not wanting to acknowledge that it included the death of my child.

Too many times I said, *Yes,* when I wanted to tell my child *No,* he couldn't go on that trip, or to the movies with a friend, or to the concert, or cliff diving. I imagine that I am no different from the millions of other parents, including Natalee's, who want so badly to protect their children, yet understand they need to allow their children to experience life.

As a mother, I had done my best to teach Chris right from wrong and all of the normal cautionary things we as parents share with our children. As I look back, I'm glad he got to experience all of those things and more.

At the time, I did the only thing I could to stay sane—I prayed to God to keep my child safe and trusted that He was in control. While some of you might think God let me down, I never once had that thought. Allowing God to carry my burden of *knowing* and the outcome allowed me to be able to let Chris lead his life the way he chose. It also allowed me to participate in the lives of my other children without hanging on for dear life that something might happen to them too.

Now that I am aware of the pre-birth planning that both Dr. Mary Neal, Betty Eadie and RaNelle Wallace discovered during their near-death experiences, I understand where the adage, "It was God's plan" comes from. What they fail to add was that it was also *our* plan.

We designed and agreed to it.

That was a challenging idea to wrap my head around; the thought that my son and I had predetermined his death. But the evidence was there if I chose to acknowledge it. When I did, it helped remove the guilt I felt for not being able to prevent the accident and allowed me to look for the lesson and the gift in the experience. I still felt the deep pain of my son's death and absence, but soon discovered that choosing gratitude got me moving forward again on my healing journey.

The Lesson and the Gift

Grief can be an opportunity for a profound personal transformation. When we look for the lesson and the gift in a life challenge, the energy of the experience begins to change. We begin to increase our vibration. This vibration creates a rippling effect that permeates all areas of our lives. As we shift our perception of a particular experience, we realize that our reaction to it also shifts, even loss.

Choosing to feel grateful about something during my grief journey helped to raise my vibration and affected not only the experiences I began to have, but also the people I met with during this time. I noticed that when I was deep in grief and my vibration was low, people avoided me. I couldn't blame them. That kind of energy and situation is challenging to be around for anyone who had not lost a loved one. I certainly wasn't enjoying the experience. When I shifted my focus to gratitude, those same people responded differently to me. We were act and communicate about my loss and I was no longer avoid.

ple are at a loss for what to do and say when someone dies. The death of a child is so devastating people would rather not think about it or accidently say something to make us feel worse. I definitely heard some zingers like, "Now, Virginia, you have three other children." While the statement took me aback, I also recognized the opportunity to focus on their intention to make me feel better, instead of the inappropriate words that came out of their mouth.

By focusing on the positive, no matter what the situation, I was able to increase my vibration and begin my healing journey. Viewing my son's death from the victim's perspective 's' served no purpose other than to hold me in the lower vibration of pain and despair and make me and those around me miserable.

Thus 's' became a roadblock to my healing. I did a great disservice to my son, my family and myself by spending time feeling regretful and guilty—beating myself up for things I should have done differently and feeling like a victim. In fact, I asked myself if I had been the one to cross over first, would I want my child to feel guilty, regretful and wallow in despair. I would much rather have him discover the lesson and the gift in the experience and use the information to aid in his healing.

Let me also add that we are allowed to wallow in our experience and express our grief as long as we want. It is our grief. Once again, there are no definitive road maps for grief and each journey is unique. I am just sharing what I noticed during my journey and what helped with my healing.

By clinging to the notion I somehow had the power to change the outcome, I did a disservice to myself, especially in light of the startling information we have about pre-birth contracts, premonitions, near-death experience and our participation in a predetermined life plan. I discovered that resisting my own lessons caused me pain. When I looked for the lesson and the gift in my experience, it eased my pain because it changed my perception of the event. I learned everything is a choice, even how we choose to see and experience.

When I shifted my thinking to gratitude 'S' instead of regret 's', I raised my own vibration as well as the vibration of others around me. I was grateful for all the time I spent with my son when he was here with me physically and cherished the wonderful memories I hold in my heart. I was also thankful for my beautiful grandson Logan and the opportunities that arose from this tragedy, including the awareness of the things I would have done differently.

I am grateful that I have been able to embrace the concept of a soul contract or plan, and that Chris's death was part of an agreement we made before birth. I am grateful that I was able to open myself to Spirit and the remarkable experiences that followed. All of these things helped to reframe my grief, ease my pain and suffering, and aid in my grief healing.

Natalie

Natalie Sudman is the author of *Application of Impossible Things*. She was a civilian employee of the Army Corps of Engineers who suffered near fatal injuries and an NDE when she was blown up in a roadside bomb in Iraq. During her NDE, Natalie was able to see a broader picture of how her extensive injuries offered her an opportunity for greater awareness. She says:

> I may be in unpleasant circumstances, but my conscious mind's joy is understood as a choice that can only be destroyed by my choice of perspective. I can choose to view myself as a victim of circumstance or as a creative investigator and cooperative partner. I can choose to view my circumstance as random and meaningless or find and create the meaning in them.
>
> My joy need not be destroyed by losing the sight in one eye. My joy is destroyed by *believing that it can affect my joy*, thereby making it so. The moment I become aware of myself

as a Whole Self, I ceased to be a victim of anything. Instead, I become the cooperative creator of my own experience, fully responsible. It's possible to change my trajectory by changing my thoughts.[90]

It was extremely challenging to feel the deep pain of Chris's sudden death and absence and embrace a new perspective and the information I'd discovered. However, if I accepted that I was a willing participant in a pre-birth plan with my son, and both he and I had chosen this experience, how then could I continue to see either my son or myself as victims? Shouldn't I instead seek the lesson and gift in the experience and use them to aid in my healing?

What was the reason for Chris's early death? What opportunity for growth or spiritual evolvement did it give me? What was the take away from this tragedy? How could I choose to view my circumstance with meaning?

If I accepted the overwhelming evidence that we live on after the death of our physical bodies, confirmed by Eben Alexander, George Rodonaia and Harry Hone who returned with information only available through the survival of consciousness outside their body, then how can I continue to believe that I am separate from Chris or that I have somehow *lost* him?

Julia Assante, Ph.D., author of *The Last Frontier: Exploring the Afterlife and Transforming our Fear of Death* says, "A moment on the other side of death's door is the most powerful transformative event there is in a life outside of birth. It is the ultimate conversion, utterly without hype. It is there we watch our greatest fears collapse into nothing."[91]

If I no longer cling to the perceived belief of separation and loss, my fear surrounding the death of my son dissolves into nothing. If I embrace the idea of life after death and the survival of my son's consciousness completely, then I must eliminate the fear of loss and separation surrounding traditional grief.

Fear is the foundation that creates the suffering during is inevitable. Someone we loved has died. But is our perce death creating our suffering? What if we discovered that we had the power to change our perception of death? Wouldn't this also have the power to change our grief?

It was possible to feel both gratitude and pain regarding Chris's absence even while giving myself permission to heal and participate with joy and happiness in the lives of my remaining children. By shifting my perception of death from finality to eternity, I am living life from Source, effecting positive change in the world and giving myself permission to heal my grief. Because of this I did not let my son's death define me; I let it inspire me.

Now I have the opportunity to move forward and make those changes with my children, friends and family. I am determined to do my best and live without guilt, regret, sadness and despair, all because of the lessons learned from my son's death. I do slip from time to time, but I pull myself back up as soon as I can and continue on my journey of Source, Spirit and Self.

During this process, I discovered something interesting. Through the years as I prepared for my son's early departure, I assumed that if I was spiritual enough, I would be able to move through grief and return to my "normal" life. This wasn't as easy as I had hoped. I could never have predicted the amount of physical and emotional pain I would experience when Chris finally transitioned.

Although I had some control over my perception, my physical body rebelled. In the midst of my grief, I became forgetful and unable to concentrate. I cried at inconvenient times and sometimes for reasons seemingly unrelated to my son. As life took on a completely new dimension, the normal everyday things I used to focus on and worry about seemed to disappear. I was experiencing transformation on a deep level.

After Chris's death, it took me two years to return to some semblance of normalcy. Had I also been surrounded by support from family and friends who understood that we are eternal beings with pre-birth contracts, I believe my grief healing would have begun much more quickly.

My personal experiences and newfound knowledge gave me the ability to control to a large extent how I grieved, because I was able to embrace the idea of pre-birth contracts, NDE, past lives, reincarnation, premonitions and other spiritually transformative experiences (STEs). With these tools, I was able to reframe my grief experience.

Personally, grief made me feel bad while Spirit made me feel good. Why couldn't I grieve feeling good, or at least, better than miserable? Was I bound to follow cultural dictates or was another way possible?

CHAPTER TWELVE

"When we lift our perceived limitations off the traditional grief experience, we lift our perceived limitations off our ability to heal."
~ Virginia Hummel

Permission to Heal

In 1999, seven years before my son's death, I read Eckhart Tolle's, *The Power of Now: A Guide to Spiritual Enlightenment.* He says, "As long as you make an identity for yourself out of the pain, you cannot be free of it."[92] This was an intriguing idea as I had many painful life experiences, including three divorces in my 20s. Experiencing infidelity, along with verbal and physical abuse weighed heavy on my heart, as I had dragged my children through that too.

Frankly, it took a bit of practice but once I identified how to step outside of my "pain-body"[93] and view the drama I had experienced with non-judgment and an opportunity to learn, I immediately felt relief. As long as I held onto the victim identity, I felt pain. When I claimed responsibility for my participation for my greater spiritual awareness, I no longer needed to look outside myself either to blame someone else or to find my happiness.

Natalie Sudman was caught in a roadside bomb attack in Iraq. She discovered something interesting during her near-death experience and says:

I want to give others a glimpse of the expanded perspective that I experienced in order to assure them that their pain isn't forever, there is value and reason in it, and that the reason is their own—the experience is potentially as valuable as their pain is intense and real.

Acknowledging that life can be utterly miserable and difficult, I'm suggesting that sometimes joy can be found even within and between difficult experiences. The way we think about the experience can transform it in surprising ways. By becoming aware that on some level, we created this experience and that it's valuable to our Selves, a new perspective can be gained that may shift our emotions and thoughts regarding physical life experiences.[94]

My choosing which injuries to retain and my being blown up by a roadside bomb in the first place are assumed to be valuable, useful, and good from the perspective of my expanded awareness states.[95] Understanding that I designed my experience start to finish, and being assured through my experiences out of body that my life *as it is* has meaning and value, suffering is impossible.[96]

Dr. Joe Dispenza is the author of *Evolve Your Brain: The Science of Changing Your Mind*[97] and was featured in the movie *What the Bleep Do We Know!?* During a workshop I attended at a conference several years ago, he mentioned that the brain's reaction to fight or flight is ninety-seconds long. Adrenaline is released as the body gears itself for action. After ninety seconds, our fight or flight response becomes a choice that we make either consciously or subconsciously.

This is also true for trauma and memories. Once the initial event is over, we can learn to transform our physical and emotional response to a devastating experience. It takes a bit of conditioning but it is absolutely possible to do.

During my grief journey, I realized that when my thoughts drifted to my son, my body instantly reacted with heartache and pain. This in turn fired up all sorts of emotional and physical feelings. I began to cry, and the more I cried, the more miserable I felt. I hated feeling miserable and out of control. The crying disrupted the life I still had to live.

Not long after I returned from a conference with Dr. Dispenza, I found myself in one of those crying moments. Suddenly his words resounded in my head: anything after the ninety-second flight or fight response becomes a choice.

Was I choosing to continue to cry?

Was I caught in a cycle that I was either subconsciously or consciously creating? Could I stop it or at least lessen my response to the physical pain of my son's absence?

Dispenza also said, "Humans can turn on the stress response just by thinking about it. The chemicals of stress produce a drama in our lives and we become addicted to this 'rush of energy.' Memorized behaviors are ninety-five percent of who we are. You can un-memorize emotion. A memory without an emotional charge is wisdom."[98] I realize this is when we are able to look back and see the lesson and the gift in an experience.

In 2006, I tried to think of my son without a negative emotional charge, but I didn't understand exactly how to do it. Even though I faltered and stumbled, I always came back stronger and filled with more determination. During crying episodes, and bolstered by the information from Dr. Dispenza, I began to repeat: "Anything after ninety-seconds, I am choosing to do."

Allowing myself to explore my thoughts and feelings as I cried, I realized two important things:

1. Allow myself to grieve.

Grief is normal. Crying is normal. I am sad that my son is gone. I miss him. However, I also realized that fear was a big part of my grief: fear of separation; fear of not knowing where he was and whether he was safe; fear he's gone forever. There were also visions of the accident scene and thoughts of his physical and emotional pain, the missed milestones and the guilt because I wasn't there to help him. These tremendously powerful thoughts caused powerful physical and emotional reactions in my body. The second thing I realized:

2. Become aware of the moment when I recognize myself grieving.

A baby cries without knowing why. She reacts instantly to pain, hunger and need. At first, I reacted to the loss of my son without thought. Then eventually I became aware of the thoughts of separation, loss, his perceived pain and my guilt *that caused me to react*. This is when I had an *opportunity to choose* to continue with my pain or begin to step out of the "pain body."[99]

It is the moment I recognize a thought creates a reaction.

When I recognized what I was doing, I could consciously begin to choose my experience by choosing my thoughts. This includes recognizing my experience with greater spiritual awareness and without judgment. I felt like I was in a washing machine on "agitate" with my emotions trying to find my balance through this process, but it worked.

Although I attempted to filter my thoughts from the very beginning, I was navigating in uncharted waters. Like a ship without a compass, I knew where I wanted to go, but had no directions for getting there, and no support. Vaguely, I had remembered reading Tolle's book in 1999 and his idea of stepping outside the "pain-body."

It was a great theory and it worked when I applied it to my divorces and other painful life events. But could I apply that concept to the death of a child?

As the creator of my grief journey, I knew if I thought about the accident I would feel horrible and cry. Sometimes I did it anyway. I just wanted to feel it and roll around in the "pain-body." In his lecture, Dr. Dispenza said we can become addicted to the "rush of energy" we get from memories. I definitely felt the emotional and physical rush from those memories the instant I had the thoughts.

Louis LaGrand, Ph.D., author of *Love Lives On* says, "What you think and do causes what you feel, good or bad. Emotions don't just appear; we think them into existence!"[100] He also says that negative emotions are stronger than positive ones and it takes a concerted effort to take action and want to change them. But it is possible.

As I continued to practice shifting my thoughts from negative to positive, I noticed the most wonderful thing began to happen. Each time I was rewarded by feeling so much better. When I felt better, I was able to recognize the presence of Spirit, which in turn validated my belief in the eternal nature of our soul and eased my grief.

I realized I had already practiced focusing on positive thoughts with great results when experiencing divorce, disappointment and self-doubt, so I knew it worked. However, it also took my willingness and determination to want to make a change. I wanted something more than a lifetime sentence of pain and misery. I wanted a new way to grieve, one that included the joy and happiness I received from the spiritual connection with my son.

It is important to reiterate that crying is a beneficial and normal part of our grief healing. During this process, we must be kind and compassionate toward ourselves. Grief is an individual experience. No two grief journeys are alike.

The power of my thoughts changed my energy and vibration during grief. I was able to not only relieve my suffering and pain, but also connect with Spirit, which ultimately enhanced my experiences and sensitively to orbs and other types of after-death communication (ADC). The spiritual experiences I had from an increased energy or vibration actually eased my grief process. They gave me something positive and uplifting to focus on during bereavement. My thoughts and emotions were key when trying to shift my perception and relieve my suffering.

Ten Things to Shift Your Thoughts:

1. Remember you are the creator of your grief journey.
2. A thought creates an emotional reaction. Be proactive in the thoughts you choose.
3. Remember the overwhelming evidence from NDE that we live on after the death of our physical bodies.
4. Embrace the concept that we are eternal souls here to experience greater spiritual awareness.
5. Include your newfound knowledge on pre-birth contracts, premonitions and *knowing*.
6. Raise your awareness. Consciously look for signs from spirit and the new connection you can create with your loved one. Focus on the feelings of excitement and joy from these connections.
7. Practice gratitude. Each day find something to be grateful for even during moments of deep grief.
8. Find the lesson and gift.
9. Share your experiences with those who are supportive.
10. Be of service.

CHAPTER THIRTEEN

*"Change the way you look at things
and the things you look at change."*
~ Wayne Dyer

Think + Feel = Shift

My grief journey presented the opportunity to experience wide swings in my emotions and ultimately in my vibratory levels. They were markers I could easily identify. I was either deep in grief and sadness, or joy-filled and tingling from an experience with Spirit.

When I focused on Spirit, I felt a shift in my mood and energy. This allowed me to embrace positive feelings of connection. It raised my vibration and created the opportunity for yet another experience with Spirit. Seeing and photographing orbs affected me the same way.

Not everyone sees orbs or finds joy in photographing them. Our loved ones communicate in many different ways. At meaningful times, some people may see butterflies, dragonflies, hummingbirds, feathers, pennies, or any sign that is unique to the individual who has crossed. These are wonderful everyday objects that God uses in order to let us know that Spirit is nearby us.

The following story is one example of the miracles that have happened in my life since I used thoughts to increase my vibration and my connection to Spirit. It is from my first book, *Miracle Messenger*, and reminds me of the quote from John 1:32: "I saw the Spirit come down as a dove and remain on him."[101]

Hummingbird

On January 16, 2008, almost two years after my son's death, I was in my new house unpacking some clothing in the master bedroom. The moving van had not yet arrived and only a few boxes were stacked in the room. I wondered to myself if my son knew I had moved. The spiritual side of me jumped in and I chided myself with, "Of course he knows, silly."

Instantly, I heard a strange thrumming noise. After ignoring it for several minutes, I went to investigate. A hummingbird had flown in through the open crack of the sliding door and was trying desperately to escape through one of the four large picture windows in the family room.

As I watched the bird flutter against the large glass window, I realized there was no way of guiding him down the high wall and out through the door. I certainly didn't want to traumatize him by waving my arms and possibly chasing him around the great room in an effort to send him outside. What should I do to rescue this little creature and deliver him to safety?

Suddenly, I felt compelled to walk towards him. He was still fluttering, unsuccessful in his attempt to escape through the window. Since I thought my presence might frighten him, I stopped ten feet back from the window. Then, as if guided by some unseen force, I stretched my palm into the air as high as it would go and closed my eyes.

To my utter amazement, the tiny bird lighted on my fingertips. My breath caught, my heart fluttered and time stood still. I slowly lowered my hand and gazed in awe at the tiny, almost weightless creature before me. He was magnificent. I drank in the iridescent green of his coat, his dainty head and long beak, his tiny spider-like feet, one on the tip of my index finger and one on my middle finger.

"You're beautiful," I whispered. "Oh my God, look at you."

My little friend cocked his head this way and that as if he understood and appreciated my heartfelt compliment. He appeared completely relaxed and calm as if he knew this was exactly what he was supposed to do and where he was supposed to be. I was caught up in the wonder of the moment—his presence, his beauty, the miracle in my hand—when suddenly thoughts of my beautiful son filled my mind.

Instantly, I felt the energy in the room shift as if the very air itself was charged with a strange electrical current. Goose bumps exploded on my body. Then I felt him. Chris was everywhere: in the air and sunlight that poured though the windows, beneath my feet, touching my skin.

Even though I already knew he was here, I had to ask. "Chris," I whispered. "Is that you, buddy? You're here, aren't you?"

I knew he was. I knew it in my gut and in my heart and in every fiber of my being. I knew he was behind this little miracle. Not that he was necessarily the bird, but it was his way of letting me know that no matter where I lived, he would always be with me.

My heart sang and my spirit soared. My love and gratitude spilled forth, filling the room around me. Life is fascinating and so much, much, more than I had ever been taught. As I drank in the magic of the moment, my gaze drifted back to my hand.

The tiny bird was still patiently perched on my fingertips—a miracle messenger. I felt so small and insignificant in this incredible experience, yet I was so grateful to be part of it, so grateful that as a mother I could ask a heartfelt question of my son on the other side and instantly receive confirmation that he had heard me.

Once more, I focused on the mission at hand: getting the little bird safely out the door. With the stealth of a cat, I crossed the room, the bird still perched on my fingertips. Then slowly and carefully, I made my way to the sliding door. If only I'd opened it more than twelve inches earlier that morning. Holding my breath, I prayed I would be able to slip through the opening without disturbing him.

Success! Now I was in for another surprise. Once I had stepped outside, I assumed the hummingbird would fly away. Instead, I was dumbfounded to find him still content to stay perched on my fingertips. He was looking around, but obviously waiting for something to happen.

The silence stretched between us as I studied him once again, this little creature of God, a messenger, a miracle. He continued to rest on my fingertips long enough to make me question whether or not he would actually fly away. Next, I did what any rational person would do with a tiny hummingbird perched on their fingers. I spoke to him.

"I am so glad you came to visit me today," I cooed. "You are welcome to come back any time."

We stared at each other silently for a moment. I had the distinct feeling that he was waiting for something else as he glanced around patiently and waited for me to figure it out. But what?

Maybe I was supposed to tell him it was okay to leave. I thought about this for a moment. How absurd that seemed. Yet, my intuition nudged me to speak to him again and so I did. "I'll be okay, little one. You can go now."

With that, he looked me straight in the eye, nodded his head and disappeared into the brilliant blue sky. I staggered backward a step or two with my mouth agape and my hand on my heart. What in the world had just happened?

I stood there imprinting every detail to memory, soaking in the magic and grateful for the moment, grateful for the knowledge that my son was here with me. To this day those precious moments are as vivid and real as the instant they happened.

The memory of this experience always lightens my heart and reminds me to look for the possibility of an instant miracle from our loved ones on the other side.[102]

Prior to that story, hummingbirds had occasionally appeared at my old house at meaningful times but I had never had this type of encounter with them. People asked me why my son would choose a hummingbird as a meaningful sign of after-death communication and a way to connect with those he loved. My answer came when my daughter Kristin discovered five years after he crossed that Chris's snowboard had a huge picture of a hummingbird on it.

Since I've made the conscious decision to raise my vibration through my positive thoughts, I have experienced hundreds of miracles. These miracles have helped me to *reframe* my grief experience, *reclaim* my life, and *rejoice* in my new connection with Spirit and with my son."[103]

Albert Einstein said, "There are only two ways to live your life: one is as though nothing is a miracle, and the other is as though everything is a miracle."[104] When we look at life and its experiences as miracles, we automatically raise our vibration. By choosing to see life as a miracle, our experiences become miracles.

It is possible for all of us to experience these miracles. And reframe our grief experience. It all began with a shift in my perception.

Everything is a Miracle

What does a shift in perception have to do with vibration? Ask yourself this question: which do you believe?

A. The hummingbird landed on my hand because it was tired of flying. 's'

B. The hummingbird landed on my hand because of my son's presence. 'S'

Choosing 'A'— the bird was tired—puts one into a vibration of lack. (s) Choosing 'B'— it was because of my son's presence—puts one into a vibration of gratitude. (S)

Imagine the classic concept of a half a glass of water. Do you refer to it as half empty or half full? More than being an example of positivity or negativity, half full places us squarely in the *vibration* of gratitude while half empty lands us in a *vibration* of lack: two different places of vibration with two different outcomes that greatly affect our lives.

The vibration of gratitude is closest to God, Source, I AM Presence; and the vibration of lack is farthest away from that Source. Gratitude, love, joy, happiness and excitement send a specific signal into the Universe, which attracts the same energy back to us. Lack, sadness, despair, fear and anger send a different signal. The Universe matches whatever vibration it receives, according to the Law of Attraction. If given a choice, where would you want to be?

I heard someone had asked Mother Teresa if she would attend an anti-war rally. She said no and replied, however, that she would attend a pro-peace rally. It appears as if she intuitively knew the power of vibration and how powerful one's intention can be. Anti-war has a negative frequency vibration and pro-peace has a positive one.

It is important that we recognize which direction we are coming from in our thoughts, words and actions because they affect not only our own lives but also the lives of those around us. We all have different experiences with different circumstances. Each is an opportunity to learn and an opportunity to use our thoughts to shift our perception. We can find a lesson and a gift in each experience and use it to create something good or we can choose to embrace the pain and remain in a state of despair.

My son died in an accident and I wondered if someone whose child died under different circumstances would also be able to make a shift in their perception of the traditional grief experience.

Barbara

Barbara Stone Bakstad and I met at a spiritual conference in Phoenix in 2011. We have become good friends, bonded by the death of our sons and our positive perspective. But Barb didn't lose just one son. She lost two beautiful boys. Adam was two-and-a-half-years old when he drowned in a lake while his six-year-old brother David was nearby. Years later, at the age of twenty-one, David took his own life. How does a parent survive such loss?

From the moment she realized both Adam and David were gone, Barb reached out for a connection to Spirit and an understanding of the events on a deeper level. Yes, she grieved, but she has also chosen her own grief journey and used the power of thought and the numerous signs from Spirit to guide her forward in a proactive way.

Barb says that Adam sends a butterfly to let her know he is nearby while older brother, David, sends a dragonfly. Barb still has David's iPod and says he "spins her songs" and she knows they are from him. She recognizes the messages in the words of the songs that seem to play at just the right moment.

It is wonderful the way Barb and I laugh when we are together. I am always lifted up in her presence. She does feel the absence of her boys and always will, but she also understands the power of thought and chooses to include laughter and an optimistic outlook in her grief journey. She was recently certified as a Soul Coach and helps others learn to also shift their perspective on challenging life events and live a life that includes joy and laughter.

I met Tom Zuba during the filming of my grief documentary. Tom's uplifting attitude is a result of his perspective about the untimely deaths of his wife and children.

Tom

Tom Zuba, author of *Permission to Mourn: A New Way to Do Grief* says his life was shattered at the unexpected death of his eighteen-month-old daughter Erin. It took him a long time to recover.

Eight years later, his wife, Trici, died suddenly leaving him to raise their two boys, Rory age seven, and Sean age three. Tom knew he would survive; he had done this before. Some parts of his grief journey were new and others familiar, but now his two boys depended on him. Then six years later, Rory died of brain cancer. Again, Tom knew he would survive, but he wasn't sure he wanted to. He says, "This time I realized that I could consciously participate in my own transformation. This time I was able to observe my journey... not simply feel victim to it."[105]

> I don't want to minimize where I have been. I have been in the deepest, darkest, most hopeless, indescribable pit of dark despair that anyone can imagine. Grief has been my greatest teacher. We will always have a relationship with the people who have died and when we can tap into that we accelerate our healing. The death of someone we love is an invitation to awaken. A loved one's death is not something that happens to us, it happens for us so that we may wake up.

Tom has become an author, speaker, and Life Coach. He has discovered a new way to "do grief"— a way rooted in hope that offers the promise of a new, full, joy-filled life.[106] He has turned the three tragic and painful deaths of his family members into something to help others heal. "One of the intentions I set was that I want my life to be

about hope and shining a light for other people. If I can allev
pain for some people then my mission has been accomplis'
has used the power of thought to transform his grief and make a positive change in the world.

Cheryl

In 2013, Cheryl Hammond responded to a Facebook post I made asking parents who had lost children if they had any signs or premonitions of their child's death. Cheryl replied with Jessica's story mentioned in Chapter Three. She also says:

> There is the soul part of me that understands completely, sees the bigger picture and gets it, but there is also the mommy part racked with pain, sadness and anger at times and just wants her back. It is a process as I am sure you know. I have been through all the colors of grief many times. Jessica is the one who saved me and pulled me out of the pit of darkness.

Cheryl says that after-death communication with Jessica showed her the light and helped give her the strength to do what she needed to do here in this lifetime. Cheryl also considered doing something to help change the very lax laws in Maryland regarding drunk driving, but she heard Jessica say loud and clear, *"That would only put more punishment and negativity in the world. You are there to help raise the consciousness of those stuck in the darkness. You are there to provide more Love, Light, Hope and Truth to the world."*

Cheryl now give speeches in the community about the dangers of drunk driving, helping to awaken those drunk drivers to a higher level of consciousness, and also helping others to also see their way out of the dark. She has found a way to channel the pain of her tragic experience and be of service to others thus aiding in her ability to heal her grief.

Another person who has taken a devastating event and found reason and meaning to move forward is author and speaker Jeff Olsen.

Jeff

Jeff Olsen, author of *I Knew Their Hearts*[107] had a profound near-death experience during the accident that claimed the lives of his wife and toddler son and discovered, "*I could choose to be a victim of what happened or create something far greater.*" Jeff says:

> I slipped from the nightmare of the crash into the quietness of pure nothing. I was encircled with light, a bright-white light that seemed to be energized with pure, unconditional love. I was calm. Peace infused this almost tangible light…I was not aware of anything beyond a few feet around me, but I knew I was in a different place. This was a place of joy. This was familiar. It was Home.[108]

> My experience showed me purpose and order. I knew there was a master plan far greater than my limited earthly vision. Even in this tragedy, I got to determine the outcome. I could choose to be a victim of what happened or create something far greater.[109]

> Once back home, in a moment of pain and frustration, he cried out his heartache to God. In the stillness afterward, he heard a voice. "It was not a harsh voice, but the loving voice of a Father who knew me, and knew me perfectly. He simply said, "*Choose joy.*"[110]

> I've learned that choosing joy in every situation brings gratitude, not because the actual events are always joyful, but because of what the events might teach me. What happens to us is not important, but the wisdom we gain is. I am thankful for every lesson I have learned and every sacred choice.[111]

Jeff realized it was entirely up to him how he perceived his life challenges which included the tragic death of his wife and child. He is an inspirational speaker and an advocate of leading a joy filled life. Jeff is also the founder of AtOne.com a powerful movement that provides assistance to those looking for more meaning and connection in their lives.

Scarlett

At the very early stages of her grief, Scarlett Lewis was told by a social worker—a woman who had lost her only son years before, "Scarlett, I have to tell you that it doesn't get any better. You will always feel this pain." Scarlett immediately stopped the woman and claimed her grief journey as her own. The woman had tried to seal Scarlett's fate to a life of despair because she didn't believe it was possible to heal the pain she felt. Scarlett knew that even though she couldn't control the circumstance surrounding her son's death, she could control how she reacted to it.[112]

The woman's statement, "It doesn't get any better. You will always feel this pain," was true for the woman because she has declared it and fully believed it as truth.

Joseph Murphy, Ph.D., author of *The Power of Your Subconscious Mind* says, "Your subconscious mind does not argue with you. It accepts what your conscious mind decrees."[113] When the social worker decreed that she would always feel the pain of loss, she sealed her fate to always feel it because she allowed no possibility of a different experience or outcome.

Yet if she now chose to decree otherwise, her experience would change. This is what Scarlett recognized immediately. We have a choice to decide how we will react to our life experiences, even the most difficult ones.

Scarlett learned that healing was an active process. While she had read extensively about the power of thought, she still struggled to keep herself from blame and regret. Losing a child is one of our most difficult experiences, but her willingness to remove the limits off her potential to heal really made a difference. Scarlett also employed the use of Tapping[114] and EMDR[115] to physically rewire her emotional response and move forward in her grief healing. By tapping into the nervous system using these techniques, we are able to short circuit the emotional pain associated with the incident.

When Scarlett inadvertently came across some of Jesse's toys she began to cry, but her friend suggested that they weren't there to make her sad, they were gifts from Jesse and he had left them for her to find. Scarlett says, "Her words completely helped me change my perception about it, and from that moment on, I chose to embrace each little gift Jesse 'sent' me with happiness and gratitude."[116]

Scarlett set her intention to see things differently. In turn, she has opened herself to healing through the power of thought and a shift in her perception of the traditional grief experience.

Through the death of her son, she has also discovered her mission in life. Scarlett discovered a message little Jesse had left on the family chalkboard. It read *Nurturing, Healing, Love*. They were big words for a little boy, but she believed it was an important message from him.

She realized through love and compassion, we could teach our children to turn an angry thought into a loving one and this may prevent another tragedy in the future. She has created *The Jesse Lewis Choose Love Foundation* to "create awareness in our children and our communities that we can choose love over anger, gratitude over entitlement, and forgiveness and compassion over bitterness."[117]

Scarlett did not let the death of her son or the circumstances surrounding it limit or define her, but instead inspire her. It is through acts of service that we honor our children and heal on a deep level.

Recently, I watched a YouTube Interview between Hay House CEO Reid Tracey and Dr. Joe Dispenza, author of *You Are The Placebo: Making Your Mind Matter*.[118] Joe says, "When people combine a clear intention with an elevated emotion, they begin to change their state of being…And if you feel appreciation, love, kindness and joy, there is an alteration and the heart gets highly coherent. When people's hearts get coherent, their brains get coherent." Joe says, "There is scientific evidence that people are making substantial changes...they are healing themselves by thought alone."[119]

It is the power of thought *coupled* with feeling that helps create our energy or vibration. Our vibration also helps us connect with spirit and aids in our healing. Countless people preach the power of thought, but it is important to know that thought and feeling together create the outcome.

Thinking and growing rich or manifesting the right job is one thing, but using the power of thought to heal from the death of a child was the ultimate challenge. Thought is a powerfully transformative tool that has helped to heal my grief and something that I continue to use every day.

Barbara, Tom, Cheryl, Jeff and Scarlett have all taken their deeply painful experiences and used the power of thought to shift their perception of the traditional grief experience and create something hopeful. They have taken charge of their life after loss, reframed their grief experience, and created a constructive platform on which to help others make a positive change after challenging life events. When we lift our perceived limitations off the traditional grief experience, we lift our perceived limitations off our ability to heal.

I invite you to consider that these awakening opportunities are not unique, but available to everyone. We don't need a profound trauma to awaken and reconnect with our authentic spiritual selves. We can consciously make the choice to do so when we set our intention to awaken.

Thoughts are powerful and during grief, it is important to be aware of our thoughts. They create feelings and feelings have everything to do with our ability to connect with Spirit and heal.

Here are five things to keep in mind on your grief journey.

It is Possible:

1. It is possible to get through the devastation of loss.
2. It is possible to get past the physical and emotional pain of grief.
3. It is possible to arrive at a place of balance and wisdom.
4. It is possible to discover the lesson and the gift in the experience.
5. It is possible to heal your heart to where you can live a life filled with joy and happiness.

CHAPTER FOURTEEN

"Perceptions power emotions."
~ William P. Young

Perception

It is our own perception that creates the outcome of how we think and feel. In the *New York Times* bestselling book, *The Shack*, by William P. Young, the character of God tells Mackenzie that "...perceptions power emotions. What you think is true about a given situation, and if your perception is false, then your emotional response will be false, too."[120]

Is it possible that our perception of death has been false? If so, then our emotional response to it is also false. I will reiterate that it is healthy and normal to cry at the loss of a loved one. But we are no longer doomed to linger in despair. By shifting our perception of death, we have the opportunity to shift our emotional response to it.

Emotion is feeling. It is the key to vibration. In the book, *Conversations with God: An Uncommon Dialogue, Book I*, by Neale Donald Walsh, God tells Neale that "Emotion is energy in motion…if you move enough energy, you create matter…Every Master understands this law. It is the alchemy of the universe. It is the secret of all life."[121]

It is wonderful that I can call at will the emotion of joy and excitement and feel it surge through my body in a tingling rush that literally lifts me up in vibration. I create this surge when I want to connect with Spirit, and particularly when I want to connect with orbs. I also used this technique to help shift to positive thoughts and feelings about my son's death.

We start by noticing how we feel. How many of us have walked into someone's house and felt instantly at home? We feel welcome and comfortable because it seems to be pervaded by a sense of peace and calm. How many of us have walked into someone's house and instantly felt ill at ease? It feels as if some unspoken energy keeps us from relaxing.

The comparison of the two environments is an example of experiencing different vibrations. Energy is real. It is tangible.

When we are aware of the energy around us, we become aware of how it affects us. It is like walking into the office and finding the boss in a foul mood. This low vibration affects everyone around him. If you bump into someone who is smiling, you immediately feel the higher vibration and it brightens your day. Everything depends on vibration because energy is vibration and everything is energy.

For many years, I'd known about the power of the energy field, but now I had proof of that power. I had discovered my "Get out of Jail Free" card. Vibration allows us to become the masters of our destiny.

We use vibration to create every moment of our lives: to connect with God, Source, I AM Presence, and with our departed loved ones. I use vibration to create opportunities in all areas of my life and to photograph orbs. I have also used vibration to help heal myself from grief and create a joy-filled life after loss. Furthermore, because vibration is a powerful tool that is available to everyone, we have the opportunity to heal all areas of our lives, connect with Spirit, and even photograph and interact with orbs.

When we become aware of our own vibration, we have taken the first step in controlling our life experience. When we open our awareness to the continuous presence of God and Spirit we have taken the second step. When we practice using this vibration or energy as the connecting link to Spirit, we have taken the third step. *Once we are open to Spirit, miracles happen.*

How to Raise Your Vibration

Feelings are the easiest way to begin to identify vibration. In order to raise your vibration, it is important to learn how to feel the difference between gratitude and lack. This exercise will teach you how to reframe your grief experience, connect with Spirit, and ultimately control your destiny.

Look for physical reactions in your body. When you have a feeling of sadness, grief or despair, where do you feel it? What part of your body responds to joy and gratitude? The locations of these feelings can be different for everyone.

Usually, I get a heavy, sick or uncomfortable feeling in my solar plexus when I am in the vibration of lack, fear, anger or sadness. I get a tingling feeling in my chest and heart area when I am in the vibration of love, gratitude, joy or excitement. It feels like I am bubbling over.

If you are having trouble recognizing these physical feelings, try thinking of something or someone you love. It can be a person or pet, or even your brand new car. I am instantly in the highest vibration of love when I see and hold my grandchildren. How about Christmas morning as a child? Remember the excitement and anticipation of opening your presents? You might even turn on your iPod and listen to a song you love. I like to play one of my favorite songs, "Ain't No Mountain High Enough," sung by Marvin Gaye and Tammy Terrell. Just hearing the first few notes gets my body moving and lifts my spirit. An uplifting song is easiest way to identify and immediately raise your vibration.

Allow yourself to feel this love and/or excitement. Pay attention to how and where you feel it in your body, because this feeling is the vibration that you are trying to recreate at will. Learning to recognize it is vital to being able to raise your vibration, shift your perception and become the master of your destiny. Once you get the idea of how to raise your vibration, try this exercise with something that makes you feel bad, sad or worried; i.e. your finances, loss of a job or friend, seeing the flashing red lights of a police car in your rearview mirror, getting a letter from the IRS, etc.

Notice where and how it feels in your body. Start with just the thought of something that makes you feel good, i.e. your pet, your baby, your new car, a song, getting a compliment, and then move on to holding that thought for a few moments.

It's okay to move at a rate that's comfortable for you. You don't have to hold a high vibration for any length of time; allow it to fluctuate up and down. The important thing is to become *aware of* your vibration and catch yourself when you begin to enter the state of lack. I use sticky notes with positive thoughts and uplifting quotes on my vision board as reminders. This process is ongoing for me as I still fluctuate up and down, but I am always aware of when I do it and can catch myself.

It takes twenty-one days to form a new habit. Consciously practice this for twenty-one days and notice what happens to the world around you. By practicing the following exercises, we can make a conscious effort to raise our vibration from lack and fear to those of love, joy and gratitude.

When I have difficulty moving forward into something new or challenging, I recall the quote by Chinese philosopher Lao Tzu: "A journey of a thousand miles begins with a single step."[122] Through single steps, I have not only been able to reframe my grief experience and reclaim my life after loss, I have also been able to create joy and happiness and become the master of my destiny.

Become Aware of the Physical Feelings in Your Body

1. Identify the feelings and location of gratitude, joy, excitement and love in your body.
2. Identify the feelings and location of anger, sadness, despair, jealousy, fear and guilt in your body.
3. Notice during the day what you are feeling and where in your body you feel it. Don't judge what you feel, just notice it.
4. Download and play a favorite song or two that immediately lifts your spirits.
5. Post notes around your environment as a reminder to shift your thoughts.
6. Photos can also change your vibration. I use a picture of my grandbabies.
7. Interacting with pets is a great way to raise your vibration.
8. Take notice of which people lift you up energetically or pull you down.
9. Catch yourself being critical of yourself or others and find something positive to say instead.
10. Embrace an attitude of gratitude.
11. Choose love. (Love is the highest vibration)

Outside Influences

Everything in life is vibration. When we are trying to live from 'S' we cannot dwell in 's'. Notice the TV shows you watch and then notice the content and how they make you feel. Now that you are aware of their effect on your vibrational level, you have the option to choose programming in alignment with the vibrational level with which you want to resonate.

Rajiv

For eighteen years, Dr. Rajiv Parti was the Chief of Anesthesiology at Bakersfield's Heart Hospital and specialized in cardiac anesthesiology.

He was also the founder of the Pain Management Institute of California. On Christmas Eve 2010, he suffered a near-death experience that profoundly altered the course of his life.

Following his NDE, he made a radical departure from his conventional medical training, abandoned his career, and now advocates a consciousness-based approach to healing. He also spends his time volunteering for community projects and teaching that chronic pain, addiction, and depression are *diseases of the soul.* "Things in my daily life changed too. I used to watch all crime shows and now I sit with my wife and watch the food channel."

"What is the difference between a crime channel and a food channel for you?" I asked.

He answered, "On the crime channel, I was seeing gory stuff, blood, murder, and people in distress. That's what I was attracted to. Now I am attracted to things that are peaceful, nurturing, and life giving."

Dr. Parti's experience is a wonderful example of how a change in vibration or energy can affect your daily life. I have personally shut off the television except for a few specific "higher vibrational" shows. I carefully choose which movies to watch and songs to listen to as it affects my energy.

The internet is a wonderful place to see uplifting videos, but I have now become careful of clicking on the emotionally charged headlines and watching violent, gory or heart-wrenching videos. Not only can they make me feel sad, angry or disgusted, they also stay in my mind for weeks and affect my vibration. Understanding how we are affected by these things, we realize we can't begin to uplift ourselves or anyone else when we are in a low vibration.

Because I believe in pre-birth planning, sometimes referred to as *Sacred Contracts*—I have come to realize that my eternal "family" or soul-group offers me the opportunity to practice the exercise of lifting and remaining in the vibration of gratitude. I also pick my friends very carefully.

Robert Schwartz, author of Your Soul's Plan: Discovering the Real Meaning of the Life You Planned Before You Were Born, writes:

> Each of us is a seed that was planted within our world's current vibration. When we raise our own frequencies through the growth produced by life challenges, we raise the world's frequency from within. Like a single drop of dye added to a glass of water, each person alters the entire hue.
>
> As we create feelings of joy, even if we do so while living alone on a mountaintop, we emit a frequency that makes it easier for others to be joyful. As we create feelings of peace, we resonate with an energy that helps to end wars. As we love, we make it easier for others, both those whom we meet and those who will never know of us, to love. Who we are is therefore far more meaningful than anything we may ever do.[123]

It is through vibration that we experience life. Once we understand this concept, we also understand that we have the power to create every moment of our lives through vibration.

By consciously opening my mind to Spirit and setting my intention to connect with the Divine through the use of vibration, I have been able to attract a divine experience. Nikola Tesla said, "My brain is only a receiver. In the Universe, there is a core from which we obtain knowledge, strength, and inspiration. I have not penetrated into the secrets of this core, but I know it exists."[124]

We now know that through vibration, our brains are also transmitters. Tesla only just began to tap into the Great Universal Mind, God, Source, and I AM Presence.

We don't have a moment to lose by being anything other than our authentic spiritual selves 'S'. When we stand in a place of authenticity and truth, we give others the opportunity to do the same. Only then will we see a shift in the consciousness of humanity toward love, light and truth.

PERCEPTION

We may come to appreciate how vital it is to be aware of our thoughts and vibration at this moment in time, if we really understood that it only takes a small percentage of the world's population, resonating as their authentic selves 'S', in order to shift the entire consciousness of the planet. You may be the one person needed to tip the scales.

CHAPTER FIFTEEN

*"If you want to find the secrets of the Universe,
think in terms of energy, frequency and vibration."*
~ Nikola Tesla

Manifesting Reality

Paraphrased from Adrian Cooper's book, *Our Ultimate Reality, Life, the Universe and Destiny of Mankind,* is the following: "Vibration is one of the most fundamental characteristics of the entire Universe. While the human body and our physical surroundings might appear to be solid, the ultimate constitution of anything is pure energy vibrating at specific rates according to its individual characteristics."[125]

Everything in the universe has its own vibrational rate. Rocks are dense and vibrate at a slow rate. Plants, on the other hand, are less dense and have a higher rate of vibration.

We know the human body is dense compared to its "soul." Humans can raise their rate of physical vibration through conscious eating, meditation and intention. The soul vibrates at a higher rate than the human body. As it continues its spiritual evolution with each incarnation, it begins to evolve into higher levels of frequency or vibration.

Perception is one key component to bereavement healing, and vibration is the other. We can change our vibration through thought which is a powerful tool for healing grief and every other aspect of our life. Harry Hone died from cardiac arrest. During his NDE he not only discovered the whereabouts of his long-lost sister, he discovered the power of visualization and imagination can be used to bring into being that which we desire. He says, "All power resides in imagination."[126]

If this is true, it means we have the ability to imagination ourselves healed from grief or any other challenging life experience.

How many times have you heard "you are what you think?" One of the first laws of quantum consciousness is the adage, "What you focus on you attract." In his *New York Times* bestselling book, *Wishes Fulfilled: Mastering the Art of Manifesting*, Dr. Wayne Dyer writes: "Rule number one is: Never place into your imagination any thought that you would not want to materialize."[127]

That's a powerful statement. Was it true? Had I had any experiences that demonstrated this rule?

Yes, indeed, all my life I realized I have experienced my thoughts manifesting my reality. A few specific moments immediately came to mind. For instance, there was the time in boarding school during a fundraiser when I walked past several long tables of raffle items: sports equipment, jewelry, tickets to Hawaii. As I looked at each item, I had a sinking feeling that I didn't deserve to win them. Then I spotted a small silver and turquoise necklace. This time the feeling inside was good and I thought to myself, "I'm going to win that necklace."

The feeling was a happy, satisfied feeling, combined with the instantaneous thought of *knowing* I would win the necklace. Two hours later, I stared at the silver and turquoise necklace in the palm of my hand. I had chosen the winning ticket. The necklace now hangs on my vision board near my computer, as a reminder of the power of my thoughts and feelings.

This experience repeated itself many times in my life. Soon I was able to distinguish sinking feelings from uplifting ones. I have experienced thousands of instant manifestations, but what about long-term manifestations and our ability to use thoughts for actually creating?

Single Man

When my two boys were very young, we spent one afternoon at Virginia Lake feeding the ducks. The speed limit around the Reno city lake was 15 MPH. A yellow Corvette and driver with a wide grin and a license plate that read "SGLMAN" passed by. He wasn't close enough for me to really see his features; all I saw was his cocky grin from a distance. I chuckled at the challenge of his license plate and then thought, "I bet if I met him he wouldn't be single long."

The instant that thought popped into my mind I chastised myself for thinking such an asinine thing. I was recently divorced and definitely not interested in marriage any time soon. However, as the middle child of four brothers, I was used to a challenge and that license plate was just too hard to resist. It was natural for me to have a thought like that.

One day a few years later, I was listening to a conversation my new husband was having with a friend. He was describing a car he once owned—a yellow Corvette with a license plate that read "SGLMAN."

I nearly jumped up and screamed in horror and disbelief. At the time, I was too embarrassed to relate this anecdote but for the purposes of this book, I am willing to suffer the humiliation. As I remembered this story, I also remembered the story my daughter Kristin had mentioned about choosing her parents while in Heaven.

Was our marriage a pre-birth plan? Was the moment by the lake a nudge by Spirit in the direction of this man who eventually became Kristin's dad? Could it have been the power of my thoughts? Either way I am in awe of the workings of the Universe. I have learned through years of experience that it should be treated with the utmost respect.

The Tree

Recently my daughter Olivia reminded me of my power of thought with an experience that occurred when we rented a home in Southern California in early 2003. As I stood in the living room in front of a large picture window, I peered through the lush leaves and branches of a beautiful healthy tree that blocked the view and the sunlight. I just love feeling the sun on me as it streams through a window.

For some odd reason, I recalled a story I had read ten years prior on a website. A couple had moved into a home and planted a garden in their front yard. In the middle of the garden stood a tree and as it grew, it started to shade a portion of the garden, hampering the growth of the items planted there. They weren't happy with the idea of destroying the healthy tree. One day as they left the house to run errands, one of them told the tree they wished there was some way to fix the problem. Upon their return home, the tree had split in half and sunlight flooded the garden.

At the time the skeptical side of me shouted, "Impossible! How could that happen?" Nevertheless, I was intrigued by the possibility. I'd had all sorts of unexplainable experiences happen to me thus far in my life, so a part of me wanted to believe this story.

For no particular reason other than the fact that I truly felt reverence for the tree but wished the window were clear for the sunshine to pour in, I said aloud: "You are such a lovely tree, but you are blocking the sunlight. I wish there was some way to let it stream through the window." One week later the tree split in half and fell over, completely clearing the window. Having forgotten about my request, I was upset and thought the gardeners were removing this gorgeous tree.

The homeowner came over to check the tree and couldn't figure out what had happened to make a perfectly healthy tree split in half. Neither the gardeners nor the homeowner had an answer for the felled tree. Suddenly I remembered my heartfelt request and the website story. I was stunned. I certainly wasn't prepared to claim responsibility for the tree because of the implications. How could my words, something I'd said to the tree, trigger such an event? It was beyond reasonable thinking; even the slightest possibility that it could be true was an unsettling thought.

Yet I had challenged the Universe before and wound up married to the man who drove the yellow Corvette with the "SGLMAN" license plate. These two stories seem spun from the whimsical imagination of a child, or a Harry Potter novel. How was something like this possible?

It seems impossible to explain the inner workings of the Universe, but what I do realize is that not only are our thoughts and words powerful; they also have far reaching implications beyond the limited scope of our small snapshot of life. Everything we do ultimately affects our world and humanity at large.

It didn't even occur to me that for my simple innocent request to take form, something had to give. Those who have experienced near-death and encountered a life review mention that everything we say and do has a far-reaching effect. A thought or action sets in motion a ripple that gathers speed and ultimately sweeps the globe. It appears that once we cross over, many of us may have the opportunity to examine and even re-experience the result of everything we say and do, and how it affects others.

Ripple Effect

Erica McKenzie, BSN RN, author of *Dying to Fit In*, had a near-death experience caused by long-term use of the diet drug, Phentermine.[128] At one point during her NDE in Heaven, she watched a giant boulder appear in God's hand. Erica says:

> It was bigger than the largest boulder I had ever seen on Earth. Emanating from this rock was the most brilliant light.
>
> God turned to me and said, *"You are the rock. You are the Light. The Light is of Me and I AM with you."*
>
> God let it loose and together we watched it fall for what felt like a lifetime. I repeated to myself, *I am the Light. I am the rock.* As the rock drew near, I saw a vast body of water appear. It was larger than the largest ocean and it stretched so far in every direction that there were no borders.

Into the water the rock plunged and I could feel the great force of its impact. Together we watched as a single ripple of water appeared. God said, *"Mankind is the water. You are the ripple."*[129]

When we do or say something kind, loving and compassionate, the ripple effect is paid forward, increasing the world's vibration. In our life review, we feel the love we gave and the feelings of those who received it. Likewise, when we choose poorly and act from anger, hatred, spite, or malice, these actions send a ripple or vibration outward. We also feel its effect on everyone it touches.

William

William Peters, MFT, M.Ed., the founder of the *Shared Crossings Project*[130] in Santa Barbara, California experienced a life review during his NDE and says:

> At one point during my life review, I got the chance to see where I had made poor decisions. The way I knew they were poor decisions was in the life review I could sense and feel the impact my actions had on each person. I saw myself at five years old pushing my neighbor off his bike and him crying and going home and how his mother was affected by it, and his younger sister being scared, and his father coming home and not knowing what to do about this out of control neighbor boy, Billy. I saw the depth of karma and that it does ripple out and I felt quite remorseful about that.

It is difficult to hear these accounts and not act on the wisdom imparted through them. It is our responsibility to become the change we wish to see in this world. The implications of this precept didn't hit home for me until sometime in the mid-nineties when I realized that the first thirty years of my life were going to be a bit painful to review. I was not an angry, spiteful, or malicious person, but during those years, in my ignorance I said or did things that unintentionally hurt people. Since then I have made every effort to be kind, loving and compassionate, regardless of the person with whom I am interacting. Sometimes it's not easy.

I've noted the importance of this principle when I realize that my interaction with someone in a loving, joyful, kind or compassionate way invites or "sets the vibration" for a similar response from that person when interacting with the next person they meet. Thus, I send a positive ripple forward.

Appling this precept to my experience with my son Chris, I used the power of thought to change my experience from pain and suffering to one of hope and miracles. I did not let the death of my child limit or define me. I let it inspire me to make a change, to search for answers, discover truths, be of service to others and send a positive ripple forward. It is through these experiences that we discover our greatness and in doing so empower others.

Using the power of thought has worked beautifully to reframe my grief experience and shift my perception of death. It has lifted me up and given me the wonderful opportunity to connect with my son and Spirit. It created a positive rippling effect that affects my children, family and friends.

By using thought to shift my perception of death and thus my reaction to it, I have given each of them the opportunity to experience a new way to grieve that includes joy and laughter. In the process, I have offered myself as proof that it is possible to make a shift.

Thoughts in Action

Many of us are unaware that our thoughts, words and actions can have a profound effect on each other, even those whom we haven't met. The following are examples of the effect of our interconnections.

In September of 2011, I met Patricia Alexander at a writer's conference in Phoenix, Arizona. We were instantly at ease with each other and felt as if we were old friends. We realized that we've known each other during many lifetimes and that we were both here to assist one another.

At the closing prayer of the conference, I could feel Spirit in the room. I captured a wonderful large moving blue white orb the size of a cantaloupe, near the producer of the conference and two of the guest editors. I had intended to send them the photo, but for some reason I never got around to doing so.

Patricia then decided that we should attend a spiritual self-help conference in November of 2011, also in Phoenix. It was the same producer. Patricia insisted that I not only attend the conference; I was also going to be her roommate. I couldn't tell her that I had absolutely no intention of doing either.

At the time, I had orbs on my mind, along with Wayne Dyer, who happened to be a presenter at this upcoming conference.[131] I had a feeling that he was connected to assisting me in moving the orb message forward.

A week before the conference I was shamed into buying a ticket. On the day I purchased my ticket, I got the overwhelming nudge that I needed business cards and scrambled to make them. On Tuesday morning, forty-eight hours before my plane left for the conference, I received the overwhelming message that I needed an orb website.

Tilting my face toward Heaven I said, "You've got to be kidding me. I can't possibly do that in forty-eight hours!" I knew nothing about websites and I didn't have the funds or anyone available to build one for me on such short notice—especially one with a multiple photo layout and all the explanations.

It was no use arguing with God and Spirit. They demanded action. Patricia thought I was crazy and told me so. It was up to me, so I spent the next thirty plus hours over the following two days, learning about and building the beginning of my Orb Whisperer website.

Wayne Dyer had taken up residence in my head for the past six weeks and I knew that somehow he was connected, but I didn't know exactly how he would help me with my orb message.

Wayne

Friday evening in Phoenix, as we sat listening to Dr. Dyer's wonderful keynote speech, he mentioned orbs. I nearly fell off my chair. I could feel an energetic shift in the room and I reached for my camera. I managed to capture a photograph of Wayne surrounded by twenty orbs, many of which were blue. (Photo 25)

Photo 26 of Wayne Dyer with two large blue orbs was taken at another conference. In 2012, I discovered what I believed to be a solid explanation for the orb color spectrum. I call it "The Newton Connection" after Michael Newton, Ph.D., author of *Journey of Souls: New Case Studies of Life between Lives*.[132] Newton, a hypnotherapist, has regressed clients into super states of consciousness to access their lives between lives.

Photo 25 © Virginia Hummel. Dyer with a room full of blue orbs. Please see OrbWhisperer.com.

Newton and his associates have regressed over seven thousand clients who were able to access their soul groups, guides and teachers. Within the groups, each individual soul radiated a different color, or variations of colors, suggesting their level of spiritual development. His clients' consensus was that souls who radiated a blue color were master teachers.

My intuition told me that the colors of orbs and the colors Newton's clients identified as souls were connected. If orbs were a manifestation of our soul or consciousness energy, then wasn't it possible the blue orbs, captured during Wayne's Keynote speech, were souls representative of the blue master teacher energy?

Nonetheless, it was inspiring to see Wayne surrounded by these blue orbs. I cannot assume to know what color Wayne's soul would radiate, but after listening to him that particular night, I knew he was indeed a master teacher; his message was profound. It was obvious to me as I reviewed the photo that Wayne had some very powerful friends on the other side, helping him awaken and educate the audience in that room.

Photo 26 © Virginia Hummel. Dyer with two large blue orbs. Please see OrbWhisperer.com.

The following morning I printed the photo of Wayne along with the orb photo I'd taken at a conference two months earlier, and set out to find the conference producer. Twice during the weekend, I tried to approach her: once she was unavailable and the other time she was nowhere to be found. It wasn't until the third time I tried to connect with her toward the end of the conference that it all fell beautifully into place. I unveiled the orb photo that included her and the two editors and then showed her Wayne's photo taken Friday evening.

My jaw dropped as I watched synchronicity in full bloom. She looked past me and called out to a woman across the foyer, "Have you Fed-Exed the package to Wayne yet?"

"No," she answered. "I was just walking out the door to take care of it."

The producer summoned her over and slipped my photo into the envelope bound for Wayne Dyer. I handed her my business card to include with it that Spirit insist I make.

On Monday morning I awoke feeling super-charged with energy. I felt as if I were getting ready to be shot out into the universe! I was walking on air. Something was coming, but I didn't know what. I was vibrating at such a rate, it was that "swimming in champagne" feeling I've described before. The feeling was unnerving.

In retrospect, I realize this must have been what Dr. Rick Strassman meant when he said that nearly every one of the volunteers remarked about the vibrations brought on by the DMT (N, N-Dimethyltryptamine) mentioned in Chapter Seven. They experienced a powerful energy pulsing through them at a very rapid and high frequency.

Several hours later, I was driving home from lunch when my cell phone rang. It was Wayne Dyer asking permission to use my orb photo in his new book, *Wishes Fulfilled*, just three days from his book deadline. I was stunned as my mind instantly cataloged all of the synchronistic events that had to have happened in order for me to arrive at this exact moment in time.

My experience tells me that nothing happens by accident. With passion and intention, I focused my thoughts on moving the orb message forward. Wayne Dyer was on my mind daily, coupled with my strong intuition that he was somehow connected. Had I picked up, via the cosmic ether or Universal Mind, his focus on orbs?

Then, because we were both focused on the same subject, did the Universe bring us together? Was this all part of a greater plan, a pre-birth plan, which included the death of my son as a catalyst for my participation?

My orb photograph and a link to my website ended up in a book written by a well-known and respected self-help guru. It was his first book that included the subject of orbs. The book would introduce orbs to a whole new segment of the population outside the spiritual and paranormal community. I was a part of that introduction.

Proof of Heaven

In April of 2012, I was introduced to Dr. Alexander at a conference in Phoenix. I was busy taking orb photographs of the speakers and missed Dr. Alexander's presentation. In fact, I completely missed the orb connection. Five months later, at a second conference in Phoenix, I had the opportunity to hear his presentation.

Even after listening to the story of Betsy, I didn't make the connection to Betsy as an orb until after he shared the galleys of his new book, *Proof of Heaven*. I was stunned. His experience with his birth sister, someone whom he had never met, and her appearance as a brilliant orb in his near-death experience, validated my theory, work and research that orbs are connected to our loved ones. I moved forward with full confidence that I was indeed on the right track.

Spirit had been driving me relentlessly for a reason. I had endured the raised brows, rolled eyes and outright dismissal by many academicians and others in the spiritual and afterlife fields. Thank God, I had been willing to listen to Spirit and participate in the greater unfolding plan, despite how crazy and difficult it seemed at the time.

Thank God I had listened to my intuition, my *knowing*, and the divine guidance I was given to forge ahead. What I find even more interesting from this experience is the truth behind the message imparted by so many different sages, philosophers, authors, and spiritual leaders throughout the centuries: that we are all connected. We are just beginning to understand the mystery of how that connection functions.

I reviewed the sequence of events and series of so-called coincidences, connecting the dots between my original thought and the outcome. Was the experience with Wayne Dyer an example of the law of attraction and that what I focus on I attract? Was it a vibrational level on which I was resonating? Was it a pre-birth plan where I, along with the souls of Eben Alexander and Wayne Dyer, had collectively agreed to help awaken others to the existence of orbs, their connection to our loved ones, and our life as eternal beings?

Was Patricia Alexander, who insisted I attend the November conference with her, placed in my path to ensure my connection with Wayne Dyer? Did the producer of both conferences also play a role in this unfolding drama by including my photo in the FedEx to Wayne?

Do we create every moment of our lives through our thoughts and vibration, and does the Universe respond in kind? Or is there also a greater plan that we agree to before we're born, for which we become witnesses as it continues to unfold before us?

When I realized that my son's death propelled me in this direction, I also realized that sometimes in the midst of a tragedy we cannot see the bigger picture and the wonderful gifts that may come from that experience.

By consciously choosing to view life from my authentic self 'S' instead of ego self 's', I have created a strong connection to God and His miracles. I have used my thoughts to raise my vibration and experienced the miracle of Spirit and power of manifestation. I have recognized and utilized the power inherent in all of us and consciously changed my grief journey from one of sadness to one of love and joy. It has been challenging but well worth the effort.

As I continued to explore the evidence pointing toward eternal life, I stumbled across another type of experience that validated our roles as eternal souls. It had to do with past lives and children's ability to remember them. Remembering a past life meant these children had more than one life. This also implied that their consciousness or soul survived from one physical death to the next.

CHAPTER SIXTEEN

"For all the prophets and the law have prophesied until John, and if you are willing to receive it, he is Elijah who was to come."

~ Matthew 11:13-14

Past Lives

The idea of reincarnation or being "born again" was intriguing to me. It meant the possibility of my son's survival. Not only could he have been here before, but the likelihood that he would return at some point in the future.

It also created a platform on which pre-birth contracts were possible, thus giving me a reasonable explanation of my premonition of Chris's death and the premonitions that Mary Neal, Scarlett Lewis, Cheryl Hammond, Vicky Ellis and Nancy Meyer had about their children, which were mentioned in Chapter Three.

Carol Bowman

Carol Bowman's groundbreaking book, *Children's Past Lives: How Past Memories Affect Your Child*, revealed overwhelming evidence of past life memories in children.[133] Her investigation was sparked when her five-year-old son described his own past life death on a Civil War battlefield. His account was so accurate it was authenticated by an expert historian. Her son Chase had a hysterical fear of loud noises and a chronic case of eczema on his right wrist.

During a past life regression by Norman Inge, Chase revealed he was a black soldier who had been shot in the right wrist. He remembered leaving his wife and children for war and described life in the 1860s. Within days of his regression, the eczema on his right wrist vanished along with his irrational fear of loud noises.

As Bowman studied each case, she repeatedly saw the same signs. Whenever past life memories had substance, the children often talked about them in a matter-of-fact tone. They told their stories with consistent details and had knowledge beyond their experience. They also exhibited corresponding behavior and traits, such as phobias, birthmarks or chronic physical conditions.

Could some of these same signs be exhibited when our children relate their premonitions of impending death, such as relating the event in a matter-of-fact tone, consistent detail or knowledge beyond their experience?

Although my son Chris didn't speak of a past life, he did relate to me in a matter-of-fact tone that he knew when and how he was going to die. I remember how shocked I was to hear him say something so disturbing, yet he appeared to have accepted it as if it was part of a plan.

When Mary Neal's son Willie told his mother he wasn't going to live past his eighteenth birthday, his tone and expression implied that surely she must have known the plan for his life because he and his mother had already agreed to it.

Jessica Hammond was consistent in telling her mother of her funeral plans and Jesse Lewis also displayed the same characteristics when he told his dad the morning of the shooting after he'd insisted that his parents weren't getting together to meet him in his classroom that afternoon, "I just want you to know…it's going to be okay. And that I love you and mom."[134]

Dr. Stevenson

As I delved deeper into the survival of the soul, I discovered Dr. Ian Stevenson, author of *Children Who Remember Previous Lives: A Question of Reincarnation.*[135] Dr. Stevenson collects cases of children who spontaneously remember a past life, instead of using hypnosis to verify a past life. Spontaneous past life memories in children were investigated using strict scientific protocols.

In order to collect his data, Dr. Stevenson methodically documents the child's statements of a previous life. Then he verifies the facts of the deceased person's life that match the child's memory. Using medical records, he matches birthmarks and birth defects on the child to wounds and scars on the deceased.

Stevenson describes a documented account of twin girls who lived in England named Jennifer and Gillian Pollock who were able to recall certain details of their deceased sisters' lives and identified individual toys that belonged to each of them.

The family had moved to another location after the auto accident that claimed Joanna and Jacqueline Pollack in 1957: yet on a return visit to that town for the first time, the twins were able to identify the former house where the deceased sisters lived, and led the way to a park where they used to play. At one point, their mother overheard one of the twins re-enacting the accident in graphic detail with the other twin. She would have had no way of knowing any of the details of the event that were included in her narration. Jennifer's body had the exact birthmark and scar as her deceased sister, Jacqueline.

What is also interesting is that the father who believed in reincarnation *knew* his deceased daughters would be reborn as twins and they were, exactly seventeen months after the death of their sisters.

Trutz Hardo

German therapist, Trutz Hardo, author *of Children Who Have Lived Before: Reincarnation Today,*[136] tells of a three-year-old boy who lives in Golan Heights near the border of Syria who remembers being murdered in his past life with an ax. At first, no one believed him, but eventually he led officials to another village where his body had been buried. He also led them to the spot where the murderer had buried the ax.

Coincidentally, a large birthmark found on the little boy corresponds to an axe wound found on the skeletal remains. When he mentioned his previous name, they questioned the villagers about the man's identity. They said a man with that name had disappeared four years earlier and never returned. The little boy named his killer who eventually confessed to the murder.[137]

Interestingly enough, the little boy's culture believes in reincarnation. They will search the body of a baby to discover any birthmarks or "death wounds" and then listen carefully to the child when they begin to talk about clues to their past life.

James

James Leininger is a young boy who remembers his past life as a WWII fighter pilot. His parent's wrote the book, *Soul Survivor: The Reincarnation of a World War II Fighter Pilot*. It is the story of their three-year-old son James who was obsessed by WWII aircraft.[138] He would scream during recurrent nightmares, "Plane on fire! Little man can't get out!"[139] His parents discovered that their son James was reliving the life of James Huston, who died in the battle of Iwo Jima sixty years earlier.

Little James Leininger knew the airplane James Huston had flown, the area he was shot down, the name of his ship, and even remembered and recognized crew members from his ship by name. He also knew intimate family details from James Huston's life.

What I also find fascinating is that in October 2002, James told his father that he found both he and his mother before he was born. He knew they would be good to him so he chose them as his parents. When his father asked James where he had found them, he described a famous landmark hotel in Honolulu, Hawaii known for its pink façade. James then added that he had found them one night when they were eating dinner on the beach.

As it turns out, Bruce and Andrea Leininger celebrated their fifth wedding anniversary at the Royal Hawaiian. Andrea was five weeks pregnant with James when she and Bruce had eaten a dinner by moonlight on Waikiki Beach. Little James Leininger not only remembered his past life, he also remembered picking his parents like my daughter Kristin had mentioned in Chapter Four.

Christian

Two-year-old Christian Haupt had an obsession with baseball and began sharing vivid memories of the 1920's and 1930's baseball legend, Lou Gerig. His mother, Cathy Byrd, said he blurted out, "Mommy, I used to be a baseball player." He recalled how he traveled by train and after seeing a photo of Babe Ruth stated they didn't speak to each other anymore. It turns out that Gerig and Ruth had had a falling out.

Christian also shared baseball history he was too young at the time to know. His obsession with and knowledge of Lou Gerig compelled his mother Cathy to contact Jim B. Tucker, M.D., a professor at the University of Virginia and author of *Return to Life: Extraordinary Cases of Children Who Remember Past Lives*. During an interview with Tucker, Christian proceeds to reveal that he picked his mother saying, "I picked her to be my mom, and then she got old." When Tucker asked when he picked her he replies without hesitation, "In the sky." Tucker then validated Christian's statement by telling his mother that many children recall picking their parents before birth.

When Christian sees an old photo of Gerig's mother he points to it and tells his own mother, "You used to be her." Stunned, Cathy embarks on a journey through past life regression and discovers she was indeed Lou Gerig's mother and went on to describe some pieces of jewelry she had once owned along with the family she had given it to. After the regression, Cathy locates and confirms with that family they had indeed received the same pieces of jewelry she had described in her past life regression.

Carol Bowman's son accurately recalled his life as a Civil War soldier with exacting detail, while the Pollack twins had the ability to re-enact their tragic end and identify places and objects that only their deceased sisters would have known. The Golan Heights boy pointed the way to his own skeletal remains and murder weapon, and then identified his murderer who eventually confessed to the crime. James Leininger remembered his past life as James Huston, his shipmates, and intimate family details while Christian Haupt recalls his past life as Lou Gerig.

How it is possible that these children can recall such detailed experiences if not for the survival of their soul or consciousness after death? Personally, it validated my intuition and *knowing* that my son's soul or consciousness also survived his physical death, and that the signs and experiences I was having with him were real.

I believe that the evidence of these children's past lives sets the foundation to make pre-birth contracts, *knowing*, premonitions, after-death communication, and reincarnation possible. I also believe it gives validity to near-death experience and the incredible amount of information recovered from these events.

My son Chris and Dr. Mary Neal's son Willie didn't mention a past life, yet knew they would die young. Scarlett Lewis's son Jesse also appeared to know of his impending crossing and asked his father, just a week before the shooting, how he would be able to locate his grandmother in Heaven if he died. Even Cheryl Hammond's daughter Jessica knew of her early departure and prepared for her own crossing.

It seems reasonable to conclude that these children had carried this information, this *knowing*, with them from somewhere beyond this world. To me, this meant that the souls who were Chris, Willie, Jesse, and Jessica existed before they were born in this lifetime. With the detailed evidence from the past lives mentioned above, it also implied that Chris, Willie, Jesse and Jessica would continue to exist after this lifetime. Now, there was also a strong possibility they would return at some point, taking on a completely new persona along with the potential to recall a portion of their past life.

CHAPTER SEVENTEEN

Reincarnation

Reincarnation is the religious or philosophical concept that the soul or spirit, after biological death, can begin a new life in a new body.[140] During the filming of my grief documentary, I had the opportunity to ask Dr. Eben Alexander his thoughts on reincarnation. He says:

> Understanding the eternity of the soul is also realizing that we come here many times and that reincarnation has an absolute basis in reality. That's something I didn't pay attention to before my NDE because I didn't realize that there is tremendous scientific literature on reincarnation. And it's pretty much indisputable.

During the interviews I filmed for the grief documentary, I asked several people what they thought of reincarnation and past lives.

Raymond

When I asked Dr. Raymond Moody if he had any experience with past lives or reincarnation, he answered with two interesting stories about his son and daughter who were both adopted at birth. Raymond says:

> Life after death was not anything my wife and I discussed at home with our children. In fact, it was only recently that my kids found out about my book, *Life After Life*, by looking me up in the Internet.

REINCARNATION

When Carter was five-years old, we were lying on the bed flipping through channels with the remote when I briefly landed on the National Geographic channel. Suddenly, Carter became very animated and said, "Dad, dad! That's my village!"

"What?" I asked as I flipped back to the National Geographic channel and the documentary about village life in China.

Carter could see that I was puzzled. He said, "Yeah, don't you remember? Before I came to you and mommy, I was with my other mommy and daddy and brothers and sisters in China."

He stills remembers it. Recently he stopped me in the hallway, took me aside, looked at me, and said, "You do know I came here for you, don't you?"

I also have a wonderful thirteen-year-old daughter we adopted at birth. She's had no exposure to ideas about life after death and certainly no exposure to reincarnation. She is a Native American Blackfoot. She likes to take long walks with me. About a mile from our house is a long wooden bridge. She just loves to sit on that bridge and talk.

One day out of nowhere she said, "I don't like this place."

It was obvious what she meant when she said *this place— the world*. I was startled. Normally, I try not to react to something my children say to let them follow through with their thoughts. This is something you learn in psychiatry and it leaks over into your personal life so you get accustomed to it. Sensing my puzzlement, she then said, "Yeah, when you die you just go up and be with God. He holds you there till all the people you know have died and then he sends you back as another person."

"What makes you think that?" I asked.

She drew both hands up toward her head in a sweeping motion. "*I just know*. And I was with God and God pointed you out to me and He said you have got to go down and be his daughter."

"Well, how did you feel about that?" I asked.

"I didn't want to do it. I wanted to stay with my God but He pushed me down to be your daughter," she said taking both hands above her head and pushing them downwards in front of her.

"Well are you glad you came anyway?"

She nodded and said, "Yeah."

What is so interesting about this story is that nineteen years earlier I had been sitting on a porch swing having a little day dream. We had two sons already and I thought how nice it would be to adopt a Native America daughter. I didn't even set it up as a prayer and quickly realized how unrealistic it would be. Yet nineteen years later, it came about without any effort on my part.

Raymond's experiences with his children brought me great comfort and assurance. Here was a philosopher, psychologist, physician, bestselling author, and the foremost authority on near-death experience telling me he has had his own personal experience with past lives and reincarnation with his children. It was validation that the experiences both my daughter and I were having with my granddaughter, Brooklyn, were real.

Kristin

My daughter Kristin has been a big part of my ability to shift my perception of death through my grief journey. Over the years, her experiences with Spirit and my son, along with her willingness to speak of such things, have allowed me to embrace the concept of eternal life. The most recent events in our family life lead us to believe that the soul who was Christopher may have returned in the form of my new granddaughter, Brooklyn.

Photo 27 (left) Brooklyn and Logan. Photo 28 (right) Christopher Arrington 6/16/80 – 2/4/09. © Virginia Hummel.

The skeptic in me is alive and well and I am prepared to wait patiently while we experience more signs and evidence from this beautiful little girl to determine if she is my reincarnated son. I will always see her as a new individual and honor her journey during this lifetime, unencumbered by our knowledge or speculation that she may be the soul of my late son Christopher. Yet, I do get a certain thrill when Brooklyn says, "Mama, I mean Grammy," when she talking to me.

From the moment Brooklyn was born, I have felt a wonderful sense of familiarity about her, a connection that spans space and time. I cannot explain the feeling; I only know that it exists. I see this beautiful little child as Brooklyn, yet something is so very familiar to me. Photo 27 is of Brooklyn at nine months and Christopher's son, Logan, at twelve-years-old.

To understand the events and clues surrounding our belief of Christopher's reincarnation, I am including an excerpt from my first book, *Miracle Messenger*, written from my daughter Kristin's experiences. She says:

> I have always had an incredibly deep connection with my brother, Chris. As children we would often snuggle up under the covers and talk about life and how we felt that we had incarnated on this earth for a very important mission; a mission to help save the planet, to help raise the level of consciousness of the people on this earth and usher in the new age of love and compassion.
>
> As a little girl, I remember looking at him and *knowing* that we came from the same place somewhere deep within the universe and that together we would accomplish our assignment. With every ounce of my being, I knew that he and I came here together for a very important cause and that together we would complete it.
>
> We never spoke to others about our plans, our dreams, or our connection. A deep understanding bridged our hearts and I always knew that no matter what, we had each other.
>
> However, of all the things Chris and I did share, there was one thing I had never told anyone, because even as a child I knew it was unusual. Although I loved my brother dearly, for as long as I can remember, I couldn't understand why I came into this world as his sister and not his mother. I felt that God had done a good job of putting us in the same family, but somehow things got a little mixed up and I became his sister instead of his mom.
>
> For many years, I explained away my thoughts and suppressed these strange feelings. In an attempt to make sense of it all, I told myself that I only felt this way because I loved him so much and understood him so well.
>
> As the years went by and he and I grew into young adults, our plans to make a difference in this world started to form.

We both decided that film would be the avenue we would take to reach massive amounts of people.

We couldn't wait to start traveling and making documentaries together that exposed important global issues. Our films would help bring people together and create necessary change for a world filled with love. Three days before his death I remember hearing a voice say to me, "Enjoy it while it lasts." I didn't understand the meaning of these words until the morning of February 4 when I received the phone call from my mother.

The day my brother died, I died too. Everything I had believed in and loved with my entire soul was gone in an instant. Repeatedly I said to him, "Why wasn't I on the back of that motorcycle that night with you? This was not part of the plan. We have a job to do down here. How could you just abandon me like this? What am I supposed to do now?"

A few months after Chris died I began having ADC's with him. One night in particular, as I lay sleeping, I found myself at a pool with my brother and his son, Logan. As I stood there watching them play in the sunshine and the water, Chris stood up and walked towards me.

When he reached me, he put both of his hands on my shoulders, looked me straight in the eyes and continued to repeat, "Kristin, I'm coming back. Tell Mom that I'm coming back. When you wake up, don't forget that I've told you I AM coming back. Make sure you tell Mom, okay?"

Each time he repeated this he shook my shoulders intensely to make sure I understood the importance of his message. After hearing this repeatedly, I pushed his hands off me and told him, "All right, all right, okay. I get the message. You can stop shaking me now. I'll make sure I tell Mom. I promise I'll remember."

When I awoke, I knew I had just met with my brother in an after-death communication. The clarity and energy of my encounter with him left no doubt in my mind that my brother planned to return to this earth. I called my mom first thing in the morning and told her about my dream.

I felt so grateful to have seen him again; to have touched his skin, looked into his eyes, seen his smile, and to hear him tell me of his plans to return.

Later that night when I got into the bathtub, I felt myself slipping into my same nightly routine of crying and drinking as I had for the past year. Just as the first tears started to fill my eyes, a sudden bolt of what felt like lightning shot through my body. In the same instant, I sat straight up in the tub and heard my brother's voice say to me, "Kristin, I'm coming back, and now you can be my mother."

These words brought my world to a screeching halt. Time stood still. The tears stopped. The lump in my throat softened, and everything I had questioned, doubted, cried about, feared and hated since his death suddenly disappeared. Love, hope, light, and excitement replaced them.

That moment changed the course of my life. It made me realize that Chris's death had been a part of the plan. Instantly, all the thoughts I'd had about being his mother when I was a child made perfect sense. At last, I understood. My life turned around. I had something to look forward to.

For the first time in years, I felt happy again. I told my mother about the after-death communication dream and that Chris wanted her to know that he was coming back—but I never told her or anyone else the rest of what he told me that night. I kept that between us.

As the years passed, I felt I needed to get away from work and school and take time to fully heal the deepest parts of my soul. I felt that my brother was encouraging me to go through a spiritual program, just as he had. On the fifth day of the program, I felt my brother's presence more than ever. I felt he wanted to remind me that he still planned to reincarnate and that he would be my son.

At this point, it had been three years since he'd first told me of his plans and I had never shared my experiences concerning this matter with a single soul. I didn't care to hear others' opinions about it, nor did I care to hear the ridicule others may express. It is such a taboo topic and sadly, I have never told most of my friends about my afterlife experiences. In my heart, I know that an unbreakable bond exists between my brother and me and I didn't need anyone else to validate my experiences with him.

However, after three years of keeping this inside of me, I began to feel a little crazy. I questioned myself and my experiences with Chris. Were my feelings about his return real or not? Did my brother actually communicate with me from The authentic self, or have I completely lost my mind? All of these questions raced through my mind as I drove to my last meeting that afternoon.

I tried to analyze my own thoughts and even started to question my sanity. Firmly I said aloud, "Okay, Chris. I feel like I can hear you loud and clear. I feel like you're telling me that you're coming back and that you are coming back through me. However, I also feel like a total nut case at this point because this has been going on for three years. If you are really there, if you are really saying these things to me, I need some proof. I need to know beyond a shadow of a doubt, that all of this is real and that you are coming back. So, if you're out there and you can hear me, make this happen."

After saying this aloud, I released it from my heart. I figured if Chris had just heard my request he would smack me in the face with the answer. If not, then I would need to drop it and force myself to stop having thoughts about his return.

As I pulled into the driveway, I let my request to my brother drift from my mind and I focused on the session at hand. Once I completed my hour-long session, I collected my belongings, and headed towards the door. As I opened the door to walk out, Albert, who was sitting in his chair behind his desk, swiveled around and with a certain amount of urgency, said, "Kristin! Come back. I have to tell you something."

Caught off guard I took a few steps backwards, peeked around the corner and said, "Yes? What is it?"

"I have something important to tell you," Albert said, "But I don't want it to freak you out. I'm getting a message from Chris and he's telling me that it's really important that I tell you, but you have to promise me you won't get scared."

The blood started to drain from my face. I knew that Albert had the ability to work as a medium and communicate with the other side, so that didn't scare me—but nothing could have prepared me for the bombshell he was going to drop.

He sat up, looked me straight in the eye and said, "Chris is telling me that he wants you to know that he's coming back, and that he is going to be your child…"

Like a cartoon in the movies, my jaw fell to the floor, my knees buckled beneath me, and I burst into tears. Suddenly, the silent, mystical world I had kept all to myself from childhood had became a reality. Within an hour of asking my brother to give me an answer, he had communicated with me through Albert and reassured me that what I had heard for the past three years was real. What I had felt as a child was real.

REINCARNATION

Never in my life have I experienced a moment of such purity, truth, and validation. No one in the entire world knew about the conversations I'd had with my brother and about his plans to reincarnate as my child. Yet one hour after my request for validation, Chris smacked me in the face with an answer he had been telling me all along.

As the years wore on, I felt the urgency of my brother wanting to reincarnate through me just as I had realized he did that night in the bathtub when I heard, "And now you can be my mom." Albert had also confirmed what I knew in my heart to be true but I just couldn't bring myself to have a child without a wonderful partner to help raise it.

One day when the urge to become pregnant was overwhelming, I said to Chris, "Okay, if you want to come through me that badly, you find me a house and a husband and I will have you." Three months later, I found my home and a few months after that I met Jeff. On our first date, while sitting in a booth at a restaurant, I noticed my brother's initials, C.A., carved into the wood to my left.

Was it a coincidence or was my brother hard at work trying to orchestrate his parents' meeting and letting me know he was the reason behind the man sitting across from me?

Jeff and I were a match made in Heaven, pardon the pun. Little synchronistic things began to happen. When my brother was alive, he used to regale me with stories about hawks that would appear near him. He somehow had a wonderful connection to these majestic animals.

About a month into our relationship, Jeff had gone to play golf. When he returned, Jeff said the weirdest thing had happened on the golf course. He said a hawk landed about two feet from him and just stood there and stared at him. He had never experienced such a thing with a bird before and thought it was quite unusual.

I just smiled inside. I knew it was Chris checking on Jeff. While some people may say it was a coincidence, I know in my heart that it was Chris behind the hawk landing so close to Jeff.

It was a message to me that Jeff was going to be Chris's new father. Although I knew it right after meeting Jeff, it was nice to know that Chris approved. Once again, the urge to have a baby was overwhelming.

Since the death of my brother in 2006, I have had numerous ADC dreams with Chris. Each time we connected, I knew I was here on the Earth plane and he was there on the other side. One of the first ADC's I had with my brother was when I saw Chris and Logan at the pool when he came over and shook me. He said, "Tell mom I'm coming back. Don't forget."

A month before my due date, I had another ADC with Chris. This time it was very different. It was as real as the other ADCs but this time I didn't feel the separation from him. It felt as if he were here with me.

In my ADC, I told Chris that it felt as if he were right here with me. He looked at me and said, "I'm not here, I'm there," and pointed directly to my belly. From that moment on, I haven't felt or thought of him on the other side as I normally would.

Brooklyn was born healthy on July 27, 2012 and I spent several days in the hospital recuperating. I was blessed to have a beautiful healthy daughter. As I look at Brooklyn, I felt such a familiarity about her. I can't say, "This is Chris," because Brooklyn is her own little person, but there is just something so familiar about her.

When Brooklyn was about nine-months-old, I was carrying her from the bathroom to the hallway. Brooklyn reached out and grabbed the doorjamb and stopped me dead in my tracks, then pulled us both back into the bathroom. A picture of Chris and me at Lake Tahoe hung on the wall.

She stared at the picture of Chris for a long time and smiled. I couldn't believe it. I was dumbfounded and I immediately called Jeff. He said she had done the exact same thing with him. Neither one of us had ever introduced her to that picture, assuming that she was too young to understand what she was seeing.

On August 6, 2013, Jeff was in the bathroom with Brooklyn. Just as he was stepping through the door to the hallway, she pointed to Chris in the picture and started chatting up a storm as if she were talking to Chris in the photo. She would point to Chris in the picture, look at Jeff and then look up and point to the ceiling.

Repeatedly she would point to Chris in the picture, babble away, look at Jeff and then look up and point to the ceiling. She was trying to tell us something and it clearly involved Chris. Jeff was stunned by the implications of this experience and neither one of us can wait until Brooklyn can really talk. We both know she will have so much to share with us.[141]

Just after Brooklyn turned two, Kristin shared another story with me. She was driving and handed Brooklyn her cell phone with an "Elmo" game on it to keep her occupied. After letting her play for a while, Kristin asked for her phone back. When Brooklyn handed Kristin her phone there was a photo of Christopher and Logan on it.

Kristin was dumbfounded. She later searched her iPhone pictures for the photo Brooklyn had found. Of the 2846 photos, two were of Chris and four of Chris and Logan. They were in an obscure album on her phone and she had no idea how Brooklyn could have found it. She felt it was more than just mere coincidence and this child was trying to tell her something.

At twenty-seven months, Brooklyn began saying, "Where's my motorcycle?" She has also been asking, "Where's Logan?" and expressing an unusual interest in him. She has other cousins the same age as Logan but only asks about him.

During Christmas of 2014, Brooklyn, two-and-a-half years old, got to spend time with Logan. We were standing in the master bedroom when Logan walked in. Brooklyn looked at him and said, "Logan's a big boy now." It was matter-of-fact, a statement, as if she had remembered him as a child and was making a mental comparison. Several times over Christmas she also said, "Logan's my daddy." It was an odd thing to say for a two-year-old and I wonder if she really wasn't trying to say, "I'm Logan's daddy."

Imagine the Possibilities

When I heard of Kristin's pregnancy and the pending arrival of my second grandchild, I was delighted. I was also excited because of what Kristin had shared with me about Chris reincarnating through her. Yet, I didn't want to get my hopes up or read anything into this event that wasn't really there.

Regardless of whether or not she was the soul of my son, it would be completely unfair to label this child and inadvertently affect her developing individuality. I knew how important it would be to remain neutral and allow the events and clues to unfold naturally, if that was God's will. However, the possibility of watching my son reincarnate and being awake and aware of the process was awe-inspiring and overwhelming.

During a conference in the spring of 2012, I sat next to a woman who was a medium. We were a group of twelve strangers gathered for dinner during a break. I had mentioned the book I was writing and that I was taking orb photos at the conference.

She interrupted me and said my son was standing next to her. She asked if I had a daughter. When I nodded, she said she had something to tell me, but I would think she was crazy if she did. I told her I knew exactly what she was going to say and I spent the next few minutes encouraging her to tell me. When she finally did, she said, "Your son said that he is reincarnating through your daughter within the next year." It was exactly what I knew she was going to say.

Kristin was five months pregnant. This was our fifth confirmation from strangers. I waited anxiously for the birth of this beautiful little soul, whoever it was. On July 27, 2012, I stood outside the operating room praying that everything would be fine. I watched a beaming Jeff, Kristin's husband, carry a small bundle down the hall toward me, and my heart burst in my chest. Both the baby and Kristin were safe.

An hour later, Jeff wheeled the bassinet down the hall toward the recovery room and I stopped him for a moment. There, swaddled in a striped blanket, lay Brooklyn. I leaned down to see my beautiful granddaughter and coo soft words of welcome to this precious little being. Her eyes were wide open and she was looking around. I spoke to her as if she could understand me and told her how happy I was to see her. Then Jeff gently wheeled her off to see Kristin.

The following morning, I was able to hold the baby for the first time. There is nothing more wonderful than to feel the warmth of a baby snuggled on my shoulder. It was Heaven on Earth. I was in love beyond anything I have ever felt. I softly patted her back and cooed to her but there was something I wanted to ask Brooklyn.

In the years since my son's accident, I realized that his death was actually a gift. It was an opportunity for my spiritual awakening and I realized it has propelled me on the greatest adventure of my life. I have read books on after-death subjects and reincarnation, attended conferences, met wonderful people, and researched and experimented with orbs. Through it all, I have strengthened my connection to God and Spirit. I have a million questions that need answers and I was hoping at some point that little Brooklyn would help me answer them.

As I swayed back and forth, I gently patted her back. I felt such gratitude that God had delivered her safely to us. As I cuddled with Brooklyn I said, "Grammy can't wait to hear your stories from the other side about God and Jesus, your guides and angels and the Ascended Masters." With that, Brooklyn lifted her head off my shoulder, leaned slightly back and turned her face to look at me. Our gazes locked and time stood still. Her eyes held the promise of an answer to all my questions. The expression on her face was one of disbelief that I would say that to her, and one of relief that I thought she was present enough to understand it.

I couldn't believe what had just transpired. This newborn had actually responded to my grownup speech. Newborns have no muscle coordination; their neck muscles have not yet developed. I was amazed that Brooklyn was able to lift her head and support it by herself. She had clearly responded to my statement. She knew, heard and understood what I had said. She also let me know that my long-standing belief that infants are far more cognizant and intelligent than we give them credit for is correct.

Two weeks later, as I held her on my shoulder at home, I made the same statement to her. "Grammy can't wait to hear your stories from the other side about God and Jesus, your guides and angels and the Ascended Masters." Once again, she lifted her head, tilted it back and turned to stare directly at me. This time I read something different in her expression. It was as if she were saying, "I can't believe that you get it, Grammy. But you do realize I'm just a few days old and can't talk yet."

Still in shock from watching her physically respond to my question, I decided that we would have plenty of time to watch it all unfold. In February of 2014, Kristin gave birth to Brooklyn's brother and I offered to babysit my 19-month-old granddaughter. I was delighted to spend a month with the family and became Brooklyn's stand-in mommy. Once again, I was in Heaven.

Proof

Kristin had another C-section, which required a hospital stay of several days. During that time, Brooklyn missed her mom and dad. I showed her photos on my iPhone of her parents and new brother Ryland and asked, "Who's that?" Brooklyn would point and say,

"Dada," "Mama," or "RyRy." She would always correctly identify them. This continued even after her mom and dad returned home with her new brother.

One day, while watching *Sesame Street,* she pointed to my iPhone and asked to see the photos. We went through the same routine of my asking, "Who's that?" and Brooklyn pointing and identifying her mom, dad and baby brother.

Suddenly, I had the urge to show her a picture of Chris in his tuxedo (Photo 28). She had never seen this particular photo and it took me a minute to find it. Meanwhile Brooklyn went back to sucking her thumb and watching TV. When I finally found the picture of Chris, I asked her, "Who's that?"

She glanced down and without hesitating, pointed to the photo and said, "Me." Without skipping a beat, she stuck her thumb in her mouth and turned back to the TV.

She confirmed what I already knew, yet I was stunned by her answer. I didn't speak or reply to her comment, knowing how important it was to observe the unfolding opportunity to witness a reincarnating soul without interference. As a researcher, I knew how imperative it was to keep the information we gathered from Brooklyn pure. Her parent's and I, along with a few friends and family, had all agreed that we would remain neutral, neither confirming nor denying Brooklyn's statements.

Part of me wanted to grab her and tell her how sorry I was that made so many mistakes when I was her mommy. I wanted to tell her how much had I missed her while she was in Heaven. I was aching to tell her I was so happy that she returned to this family and how deeply I had loved her when I was her mommy.

But I didn't.

I couldn't share that with her because it would jeopardize the opportunity to discover what she remembers on her own. I was determined to patiently standby to see if Brooklyn would eventually reveal more memories of her past life.

In August of 2015, three-year-old Brooklyn was getting dressed to run errands with her mother Kristin. They were standing in the closet when out of nowhere Brooklyn said, "I want to give this to my mom."

Kristin thought that was a silly thing to say since she was standing right there next to Brooklyn. So, she replied, "Well, who's your mom?"

Brooklyn stated matter-of-factly, "Grammy's my mom." She looked up at Kristin suddenly puzzled and then said, "Well, Grammy was my mom before you were my mom."

Then in September of 2015, I took both Brooklyn and her baby brother to the playground where Kristin and Chris had played as children. As we strolled past the familiar soccer field and neared the playground equipment, Brooklyn stuttered, "Grammy! I, I used to play at this park with my friend Johnny."

My jaw dropped and I stopped pushing the stroller for a moment to replay what she had just said to me. Christopher's best friend was Johnny Wilkins and they indeed played at that park as children.

~ END

CONCLUSION

Cracking the Grief Code happened when I discovered a connection to spirit and the information about life after death. It literally cracked open the boundaries of the traditional grief journey (the belief that we will never heal from the experience of the loss of a child or loved one) and allowed me to explore and experience a grief journey which included the possibility of healing from this terrible experience.

I felt joy and excitement in the midst of a deeply painful and traumatic event. The more I experienced the grace of God and the magic of spirit, the better I felt. No one told me this was possible or that I could heal from the pain, sadness and heartache from the loss of my son.

The stories and photos in this book have shown what we all have the opportunity to experience when we open ourselves to the miraculous nature of Spirit. Whether we recognize it or not, we are all connected to our Source—to the Creator, what we commonly call God. In *The Teachings of Don Juan: A Yaqui Way of Knowledge,* Carlos Castaneda said: "The entire truth is that the spirit reveals itself to everyone with the same intensity and consistency..."[142] It is up to us to align ourselves with Source so that we too may experience healing from the beauty and grace of that Spirit.

In spite of the resistance I encountered from friends, family, and acquaintances, I followed an unusual path led by God, Spirit, and my son. In doing so, the joy remained and continued to burn out my pain. A large part of my grief journey involved my connection to Spirit, and with it came my connection to orbs. Orbs offered me a visual confirmation that something of a spiritual nature was happening around me. Often my camera or video could record what my intuition told was present but my physical eyes were unable to see.

My orb photography introduced me to another dimension of life. Orbs became an important tool in transforming my grief. They allowed me to imagine a world beyond my own and imagine that my son survived in one form or another. In the midst of my grief, I was lifted and filled with joy at their presence.

When I introduced the orb phenomena to others who were also grieving, I discovered their experience was similar to mine. The presence of orbs provided relief, joy and comfort during a very challenging time of their life. My connection with orbs created a crack for the light to pour in and it has helped me to shift my perception of death and transform my grief journey.

Orbs became the catalyst for my research and journey into the afterlife to uncover the workings of a divine plan—a pre-birth plan that my son's early death was not random. Combined with the overwhelming information from near-death experiences, pre-birth contracts, past lives, reincarnation, and after-death communication, orbs became a tool to aid in my healing and to discover the eternal nature of our souls. The beautiful mystery of these luminous images can allow us to suspend our disbelief for a time, perhaps just long enough to consider the profound mysteries surrounding eternity and the afterlife.

Unfortunately, many of us have become victim to our grief, believing that it is impossible to heal from such devastating loss. The truth is that we can heal. First, by setting our intention to do so and then by embracing the spiritual component of the death process and afterlife that has long since been taboo. When we do, we open ourselves up to an entirely different experience than that of the traditional grief journey.

It is through the orb phenomenon and other Spiritually Transformative Experiences (STEs) that we can receive healing and validation that we survive death. We can use that knowledge and experience to help alleviate the pain caused by loss and the illusion of separation and begin to proactively comfort and heal ourselves.

We have the choice to create the grief experience we want. When we lift our perceived limitations off the traditional grief experience, we also lift our perceived limitations off our ability to heal. By opening ourselves to the miracle of Spirit and shifting our perception of death, we can experience our grief journey in a more proactive, uplifting and positive way. We *can* heal our grief.

Photo 29. A streaking orb in church.
© Diana Davatgar.

ACKNOWLEDGEMENTS

I would like to extend my sincerest gratitude to God, Spirit, and all of the following people in their effort to help me bridge the gap between Heaven and Earth:

To my son Christopher who has worked diligently from the other side to open doors and assemble stories, photos and people to help move this message of comfort and hope forward.

To my granddaughter, Brooklyn, for showing me the eternal nature of our souls. *You make my heart sing!*

To my daughter, Olivia, thank you for your wisdom, patience, love and understanding, and my daughter, Kristin, for bravely sharing your journey with Spirit.

To Erica McKenzie, Earth angel who appeared at the perfect moment. "Dorothy, the journey wouldn't have been the same without you."

To Peter Shockey, thank you for your dedication, time, energy and inspiration to help me fine-tune this manuscript and message. Your insights were invaluable.

To John Audette, co-creator of Eternea.org, keeper of the light and a vision for a better world, your dedication and perseverance to this noble cause inspires me.

Thank you, Carol Adler, Patricia Alexander, Sherie Early, Dr. Jane Early and Linda Spaeth for your edits and insights. My special thanks to Sherie and Patricia for listening and encouraging me when the mountain seemed too high. I'd like to express a very special thank you to Linda Spaeth for tackling a monumental proofreading at the last moment. I am forever grateful for your generosity and that long detailed list of corrections.

Thank you, Dr. Jeffery Long for graciously sharing some of the incredible NDE stories from your website NDERF.org.

ACKNOWLEDGEMNTS

I am eternally grateful to the photographers whose generosity allowed me to share spectacular photos of this incredible phenomenon; Diana Davatgar, Naomi Fugiwara, Nancy Myers, Patricia Alexander and Carol Danforth.

I am also eternally grateful to all the brave, beautiful souls who stepped forward and shared their inspiring stories of loved ones, Spirit and orbs. As my dear friend Erica McKenzie says, "It is only when we come together that we can do great things."

Life *is* eternal.
Imagine the possibilities!

Virginia

Reading List

Along with the books listed in the Bibliography, please also consider reading these:

Greaves, Helen. *Testimony of Light: An Extraordinary Message of Life After Death.* New York, NY, Tarcher/Penguin, 2009
(One of my favorites.)

LaGrand, Louis. *Love Lives On: Learning from the Extraordinary Encounters of the Bereaved.* New York, Berkley Books, 2006.

Spencer, Christine. *Pathways to Peace: Understanding Death and Embracing Life.* Bloomington, Indiana, Balboa Press, 2011.

Ragan, Lyn. *Signs From The Afterlife: Identifying Gifts from the Other Side.* 2015.

Buhlman, William. *Adventures in the Afterlife.* Millsboro, DE: Osprey Press, 2013
(Fantastic book for out of body experiences and includes the *most* in depth map of heaven and what happens on the other side.)

Shockey, Peter. *Miracles, Angels and Afterlife: Signposts to Heaven.* Open Road Media, 2014 (Kindle)

Heinze, Sarah. *We Lived in Heaven: Spiritual Accounts of Souls Coming to Earth.* Spring Creek Book Company, 2006

BIBLIOGRAPHY

Alexander, Eben. *Proof of Heaven: A Neurosurgeon's Near-death Experience and Journey into the Afterlife.* New York: Simon and Schuster, 2013.

Anderson, Joan Wester. *An Angel to Watch Over Me: True Stories of Children's Encounters with Angels.* New York: Ballantine Books, 2003

Assante, Julia. *The Last Frontier: Exploring the Afterlife and Transforming Our Fear of Death.* New World Library, 2012.

Atwater, P.M.H. *Beyond the Light: What Isn't Being Said About Near-death Experiences, From Visions of Heaven to Glimpses of Hell.* Transpersonal Publishing, 2009.

Atwater, P.M.H. *Near-Death Experiences, The Rest of the Story: What They Teach Us About Living and Dying and Our True Purpose.* Hampton Roads Publishing, January 9, 2009.

Bowman, Carol. *Children's Past Lives: How Past Memories Affect Your Child.* Bantam, 1998.

Castaneda, Carlos. *The Teachings of Don Juan: A Yaqui Way of Knowledge.* University of California Press, 2008.

Cooper, Adrian P. *OurUltimateReality.com/vibration-a-fundamental-characteristic-of-energy.html 1*, page 31.

Dougherty, Ned. *Fastlane to Heaven: Celestial Encounters that Changed my Life.* Hampton Roads, 2001.

Dyer, Wayne, Ph.D. *Wishes Fulfilled.* Hay House, Inc., Carlsbad, CA, 2012.

Eadie, Betty J., *Embraced by the Light*, New York: Bantam, 1994.

Famoso, Louis. www.loufamoso,tripod.com

Gleny, Mya. *Orbs: The Gift of Life.* CreateSpace (Amazon), 2012.

Greaves, Helen. *Testimony of Light: An Extraordinary Message of Life After Death.* New York: Tarcher/Penguin, 2009.

Grof, Stanislav. *The Adventure of Self Discovery: Dimensions of Consciousness and New Perspectives in Psychotherapy and Inner Exploration.* State University of New York Press, 1988.

Guggenheim, Bill and Judy. *Hello From Heaven: A New Field of Research-After-Death Communication Confirms That Life and Love Are Eternal.* New York: Bantam, 2012. www.After-Death.com

Hall, Katie, Pickering, John. *Beyond Photography: Encounters with Orbs, Angels and Mysterious Light-Forms.* 6th Books, October 10, 2006.

Hardo, Trutz. *Children Who Have Lived Before: Reincarnation Today.* C.W. Daniel, 2004.

Heinemann, Klaus and Heinemann, Gundi. *Orbs: Their Missions and Messages of Hope.* Carlsbad: Hay House, Inc. 2010.

Hone, Harry. *The Light at the End of the Tunnel.* American Biographical Center, June 1985.

Hummel, Virginia. *Miracle Messenger: Signs from Above, Love from Beyond.* Palm Desert: StarChild10 Publications, 2011.

Kagan, Annie. *The Afterlife of Billy Fingers: How My Bad Boy Brother Proved to Me There's Life After Death.* Hampton Roads, 2013.

LaGrand, Louis. *Love Lives On: Learning from the Extraordinary Encounters of the Bereaved.* New York, Berkley Books, 2006.

Ledwith, Míceál and Heinemann, Klaus. *The Orb Project.* New York: Simon & Schuster/Atria/Beyond Words, 2007.

Ledwith, Míceál. *Orbs: Cues to a More Exciting Universe* (DVD)

Leininger, Bruce; Leininger, Andrea; and Gross, Kenn. *Soul Survivor: The Reincarnation of a World War II Fighter Pilot.* Grand Central Publishing, 2010.

Lewis, Scarlett and Stoynoff, Natasha, *Nurturing, Healing, Love: A Mother's Journey of Hope and Forgiveness.* Carlsbad: Hay House, Inc. 2012

McKenzie, Erica , *Dying to Fit In*, CreateSpace (Amazon.com), 2015.

Melchizedek, Drunvalo. *Serpent of Light: Beyond 2012*. New York: Red Wheel/Weiser 2008.

Megre, Vladimir. *The Ringing Cedars of Russia - Book 2*. Ringing Cedars Press, 2008.

Moorjani, Anita. *Dying to Be Me: My Journey from Cancer, to Near Death, to True Healing*. Carlsbad: Hay House, Inc., March, 2012. www.anitamoorjani.com

Neal, Mary C. *To Heaven and Back: A Doctor's Extraordinary Account of Her Death, Heaven, Angels, and Life Again*. Water Book Press, 2012. 98, 149- 150, 151, 174

Newton, Michael. *Destiny of Souls*. Llewellyn, 2005.

Newton, Michael. *Journey of Souls*. Llewellyn, 2010.

Olsen, Jeff. *I Knew Their Hearts*. Springville, Utah: Plain Sight Publishing, 2012.

Our Ultimate Reality website: http://www.ourultimatereality.com/vibration-a-fundamental-characteristic-of-energy.html

Puryear, Anne. *Stephen Lives: His life, Suicide and Afterlife*. New Paradigm Press, 1992.

Richelieu, Peter. *A Soul's Journey*. Ariel Press, 2011.

Sabom, Michael. *Light and Death*. Zondervan, 1998.

Serdahely, W.J. *Variations from the Prototypic Near-Death Experience, Journal of the Near-Death Studies 13*, (1995): 185-196.

Schwartz, Robert. *Your Soul's Gift: The Healing Power of the Life You Planned Before You Were Born*. Whispering Winds Press, 2012.

Schwartz, Robert. *Your Soul's Plan: Discovering the Real Meaning of the Life You Planned Before You Were Born*. North Atlantic Books, May 18, 2010.

Shockey, Peter. *Reflections of Heaven: A Millennial Odyssey of Miracles, Angels, And Afterlife*. New York: Doubleday, 1999.

Steiger, Brad. *One with the Light: Authentic Near-Death Experiences that Changed Lives and Revealed the Beyond*. New York: Signet, 1995.

Stevenson, Ian. *Children Who Remember Previous Lives: A Question of Reincarnation.* Charlottesville: University Press of Virginia, 1987.

Strassman, Rick. *DMT: The Spirit Molecule: A Doctor's Revolutionary Research into the Biology of Near-Death and Mystical Experiences.* Park Street Press, 2000.

www.amazon.com/DMT-Molecule-Revolutionary-Near-Death-Experiences/dp/0892819278, pg. 123.

http://en.wikipedia.org/wiki/Dimethyltryptamine, pg. 24.

Sudman, Natalie. *The Application of Impossible Things.* Huntsville, Arkansas: Ozark Mountain Publishing, 2012

Swanson, Claude. *Life Force, The Scientific Basis: Breakthrough Physics of Energy Medicine, Healing, Chi and Quantum Consciousness.* Tucson, AZ: Poseidia Press, 2011.

Swanson, Claude. *The Synchronized Universe: New Science of the Paranormal.* Tucson, AZ: Poseidia Press, 2009.

Tolle, Eckhart. *The Power of Now: A Guide to Spiritual Enlightenment.* Navato, CA: Namaste Publishing and New World Library, 1999.

Wallace, RaNelle; Taylor, Curtis. *The Burning Within.* Gold Leaf Press, 1994.

Walsh, Neale Donald, *Conversations with God: An Uncommon Dialogue, Book I.* New York: G. P. Putnam Sons, 1996.

Virtue, Doreen. *Archangels and Ascended Masters: A Guide to Working and Healing with Divinities and Deities.* Carlsbad: Hay House, Inc. 2004.

Young, William, P. *The Shack.* Windblown Media, 2007.

ENDNOTES

Chapter One

[1] Brad Steiger, *One with the Light: Authentic Near-Death experiences that Changed Lives and Revealed the Beyond.* New York: Signet, 1994.
[2] Ibid., 61.

Chapter Two

[3] http://after-death.com
[4] Bill and Judy Guggenheim, *Hello From Heaven!* (New York : Bantam, 1995).

Chapter Three

[5] Scarlett Lewis, Natasha Stoynoff, *Nurturing, Healing, Love: A Mother's Journey of Hope and Forgiveness* (Carlsbad: Hay House, Inc. 2013)
[6] Ibid., 4,5.
[7] Ibid., 15,16.
[8] Ibid., 58.
[9] Ibid., XX.
[10] Mary C. Neal, *To Heaven and Back: A Doctor's Extraordinary Account of Her Death, Heaven, Angels and Life Again* (Colorado: WaterBrook, 2013).
[11] Ibid., 98.
[12] *Roller skiing* is a non-snow equivalent to cross-country skiing.
[13] Ibid., 151.
[14] Ibid., 174.
[15] http://treasureboxes.org/
[16] Ari Hallmark, Lisa Reburn, *To Heaven: After the Storm*(InstantPublisher.com 2012) Prologue
[17] Jeff Olsen, *I Knew Their Hearts* (Springville, Utah: Plain Sight Publishing, 2012).
[18] Ibid., 22.
[19] Helen Greaves, *Testimony of Light: An Extraordinary Message of Life After Death* (New York: Tarcher/Penguin, 2009).
[20] Ibid., 81,82

Chapter Four

[21] Betty Eadie, Curtis Taylor, *Embraced by the Light* (New York : Bantam, 1994).
[22] RaNelle Wallace, Curtis Taylor, *The Burning Within*. (Carson City, Gold Leaf Press 1994).
[23] Ibid., 115.
[24] http://www.nderf.org/NDERF/NDE_Experiences/nicola_e_friend_other.htm
[25] Betty Eadie, Curtis Taylor, *Embraced By the Light* (New York, Bantam 1994), 89.
[26] Ibid., 92.

Chapter Three

[27] Mary C. Neal, *To Heaven and Back: A Doctor's Extraordinary Account of Her Death, Heaven, Angels and Life Again* (Colorado: WaterBrook, 2013), 149-150.
[28] Brad Steiger, *One With The Light* (Signet, 1994), 72.

Chapter Five

[29] Mícheál Ledwith, Klaus Heinemann, *The Orb Project*, (New York: Atria, 2007).

Chapter Six

[30] Klaus and Gundi Heinemann, *Orbs: Their Mission and Messages of Hope* (Carlsbad: Hay House, Inc. 2011), 7.
[31] http://www.brainyquote.com/quotes/quotes/j/josephcamp384345.html
[32] Klaus and Gundi Heinemann, *Orbs: Their Mission and Messages of Hope* (Hay House, Inc., Carlsbad, CA, 2011), 6.
[33] Patricia Alexander, Michael Burgos, *The Book of Comforts* (Templeton: Blue Epiphany, 2005).
[34] The molecule DMT (N,N-Dimethyltryptamine) is a psychoactive chemical that causes intense visions and can induce its users to quickly enter a completely different "environment" that some have likened to an alien or parallel universe.
http://sprott.physics.wisc.edu/pickover/pc/dmt.html
[35] http://www.tokenrock.com/explain-third-eye-83.html
http://personaltao.com/taoism-library/shamanic-teachings/about-visions/what-is-the-third-eye/
[36] Ibid.
[37] http://balancechakra.com/?CategoryID=548&ArticleID=821

[38] http://www.tokenrock.com/explain-third-eye-83.html
[39] The pineal gland is a tiny organ in the center of the brain that played an important role in Descartes' philosophy. He regarded it as the principal seat of the soul and the place in which all our thoughts are formed. http://plato.stanford.edu/entries/pineal-gland/
[40] http://johnsarkis.hubpages.com/hub/Descartes-Concept-of-The-Soul
[41] Op Cit. http://sprott.physics.wisc.edu/pickover/pc/dmt.html
[42] Rick Strassman, *DMT: The Spirit Molecule* (Park Street Press, 2001).
[43] Strassman, op. cit., 74.
[44] Ibid., 74.
[45] Ibid, 63-64.
[46] Ibid, 146.
[47] Virginia Hummel, *Miracle Messenger* (StarChild10 Publications. 2011).
[48] Virtue, Doreen, Archangels and Ascended Masters: A Guide to Working and Healing with Divinities c and Deities (Hay House, Inc., Carlsbad, CA. 2004).
[49] Ibid.
[50] Hummel, op. cit.

Chapter Eight

[51] Max Velmans, *Goodbye to Reductionism*, "Toward a Science of Consciousness II: The Second Tucson Discussions and Debates" (A Bradford Book, 1998).
[52] Eben Alexander, *Proof of Heaven* (New York: Simon & Schuster, 2012).
[53] Ibid, 38-40.
[54] Ibid, 47.
[55] Ibid, 169.
[56] Strassman, op. cit.,76.
[57] Ibid, 146.
[58] Harry Hone, *A Light at the End of the Tunnel*, (American Biographical Center, 1985).
[59] Ibid., 23.
[60] Ibid., 27.
[61] Ibid., 141.
[62] P.M.H. Atwater, *Beyond the Light: What Isn't Being Said About Near Death Experience: From Visions of Heaven to Glimpses of Hell*, (Transpersonal Publishing: 2009).

Chapter Nine

[63] Raymond Moody, *Life After Life* (New York: MMB, INC 1975).

[64] Ibid., 36.
[65] Ibid., 40.
[66] Ibid., 40.
[67] Ibid., 40.
[68] Op. Cit., http://www.amazon.com/Beyond-Light-Experience-VisionsGlimpses/dp/1929661339/ref=sr_1_1?s=books&ie=UTF8&qid=1398028627&sr=1-1&keywords=beyond+the+light
[69] http://www.nderf.org/NDERF/NDE_Experiences/rachel_r_nde.htm
[70] Maureen McGill, Nola Davis, *Live from the Other Side*, (Ozark Mountain Publishing, 2010).
[71] Claude Swanson, *Life Force, The Scientific Basis; Breakthrough Physics of Energy Medicine, Healing, Chi and Quantum Consciousness*, (Tucson: Poseidia Press, 2010), 263.

Chapter Ten

[72] http://www.synchronizeduniverse.com/IntroductionVOLII.htm
[73] http://www.synchronizeduniverse.com/IntroductionVOLII.htm
[74] http://www.amazon.com/Adventure-Self-Discovery-Consciousness-Psychotherapy-Transpersonal/dp/0887065414
[75] Peter Richelieu, *A Soul's Journey*, (Ariel Press, 2011).
[76] http://sharedcrossing.com/
[77] Louis LaGrand, Love lives On: Learning from the Extraordinary Encounters of the Bereaved, (Berkeley Book, New York, 2006), 189
[78] Scarlett Lewis, Natasha Stoynoff, *Nurturing, Healing, Love: A Mother's Journey of Hope and Forgiveness*, (Hay House, Inc., Carlsbad, CA., 2013).
[79] Ibid., 97.
[80] Ibid., 141.
[81] Erica McKenzie, Virginia Hummel, *Dying to Fit In*, (CreateSpace, Amazon, 2015).
[82] Chakra - A spinning ball of colored energy located in one of the seven spiritual centers of the human body.
[83] Ibid., 101.
[84] Robert Schwartz, *Your Soul's Gift: The Healing Power of the Life You Planned Before You Were Born*, (Whispering winds Press, 2012).
[85] Ibid., 33.
[86] Ibid.
[87] Anita Moorjani, *Dying To Be Me: My Journey from Cancer, to Near-death, To True Healing*, (Carlsbad: Hay House, Inc.2012).
[88] http://www.nderf.org/NDERF/NDE_Experiences/anita_m%27s_nde.htm
[89] Ibid., 109.

Chapter Eleven

[90] Natalie Sudman, *Application of Impossible Things*, Copyright 2012 reprinted with permission from Ozark Mountain Publishing, Inc. Pg. 42, 43.
[91] Julia Assante, PhD., *The Last Frontier: Exploring the Afterlife and Transforming our Fear of Death,* Copyright 2012 reprinted with permission from New World Library, Novato, CA.

Chapter Twelve

[92] Eckhart Tolle, *The Power of Now: A Guide to Spiritual Enlightenment,* (Namaste Publishing and New World Library, 1999), 168.
[93] Ibid., 166.
[94] Natalie Sudman, *Application of Impossible Things*, Copyright 2012 reprinted with permission from Ozark Mountain Publishing, Inc. Pg. 44-45.
[95] Ibid., Pg. 78.
[96] Ibid., Pg.111.
[97] Joe Dispenza, *Evolve Your Brain: The Science of Changing Your Mind,* (Carlsbad: Hay House, Inc., 2014).
[98] Ibid.
[99] Eckhart Tolle, *The Power of Now: A guide to Spiritual Enlightenment* (Namaste Publishing and New World Library, 1999), 168-169.

Chapter Thirteen

[100] Louis LaGrand, *Love Lives On (Berkeley Books, New York, 2006),* 148
[101] http://biblehub.com/john/1-32.htm
[102] Op. Cit., *Miracle Messenger,* by Virginia Hummel.
[103] http://www.VirginiaHummel.com
[104] http://www.brainyquote.com/quotes/quotes/a/alberteins390808.html
[105] http://www.tomzuba.com/pages/toms-story
[106] http://www.tomzuba.com/
[107] Jeff Olsen, *I Knew Their Hearts* (Springville, Utah: Plain Sight Publishing, 2012).
[108] Ibid., 31.
[109] Ibid., 88.
[110] Ibid., 95.
[111] Ibid., 102.
[112] Scarlett Lewis, Natasha Stoynoff, *Nurturing, Healing, Love,* (Carlsbad: Hay House, Inc. 2013), 41.
[113] Joseph Murphy, Ph.D., *The Power of Your Subconscious Mind,* (Reward Books, 2000).

[114] During a typical tapping session, the person will focus on a specific issue while tapping on end points of the body's energy meridians.
http://en.wikipedia.org/wiki/Emotional_Freedom_Techniques

[115] Eye movement desensitization and reprocessing (EMDR) is a psychotherapy developed by Francine Shapiro that emphasizes disturbing memories as the cause of psychopathology and alleviates the symptoms of post-traumatic stress disorder (PTSD)
http://en.wikipedia.org/wiki/Eye_movement_desensitization_and_reprocessing

[116] Scarlett Lewis, Natasha Stoynoff, *Nurturing, Healing, Love,* (Carlsbad: Hay House, Inc. 2013), 71.

[117] Ibid., 159.

[118] Joe Dispenza, *You Are The Placebo: Making Your Mind Matter,* (Carlsbad: Hay House, Inc. 2014).

[119] http://www.youtube.com/watch?v=qxG9Rk4ufWw&feature=youtube.

Chapter Fourteen

[120] William P. Young, *The Shack,* (Windblown Media, 2011).

[121] Neale Donald Walsh, *Conversations with God,* (New York: Putnam, 1996), 54.

[122] http://www.brainyquote.com/quotes/quotes/l/laotzu137141.html

[123] Robert Schwartz, *Your Soul's Plan,* (Berkeley: Frog books, 2009), 26.

[124] https://www.goodreads.com/quotes/753175-my-brain-is-only-a-receiver-in-the-universe-there

Chapter Fifteen

[125] Adrian Cooper, *Our Ultimate Reality, Life, the Universe and Destiny of Mankind,* (Ultimate Reality Publishing, 2007).

[126] Harry Hone, *A Light at the End of the Tunnel,* (American Biographical Center, 1985).

[127] Wayne Dyer, *Wishes Fulfilled* , (Carlsbad: Hay House 2012), 74.

[128] http://www.ericamckenzie.com/praise.html

[129] Erica McKenzie, Virginia Hummel, *Dying to Fit In,* (CreateSpace, Amazon, 2015), 93-94.

[130] http://sharedcrossing.com/

[131] Wayne Dyer, Ph.D., is an internationally renowned author and speaker in the field of self-development. He's the author of over thirty books, has created many audio programs and videos, and has appeared on thousands of television and radio shows. His books, *Manifest Your Destiny, Wisdom of the Ages, There's a Spiritual Solution to Every Problem*, and the *New York*

Times bestsellers *10 Secrets for Success and Inner Peace*, *The Power of Intention*, *Inspiration*, *Change Your Thoughts—Change Your Life*, *Excuses Begone*, and now *Wishes Fulfilled* have all been featured as National Public Television specials. http://www.drwaynedyer.com/
[132] Michael Newton, *Journey of Souls: Case Studies of Lives Between Lives*, (Woodbury; Llewellyn Publications, 2010).

Chapter Sixteen

[133] Carol Bowman, *Children's Past Lives: How Past Life Memories Affect Your Child* (New York: Bantam, 1998), 8.
[134] Scarlett Lewis, Natasha Stoynoff, *Nurturing, Healing, Love: A Mother's Journey of Hope and Forgiveness*, (Carlsbad: Hay House, Inc. 2013).
[135] Ian Stevenson, *Children Who Remember Previous Lives: A Question of Reincarnation*. (Charlottesville: University Press of Virginia, 1987).
[136] Trutz Hardo, *Children Who Have Lived Before: Reincarnation Today*, (C.W. Daniel, 2004).
[137] Op.Cit.
[138] Leininger, Bruce and Andrea Leininger with Ken Gross, *Soul Survivor: The Reincarnation of a World War II Fighter Pilot*, (Grand Central Publishing, 2009).
[139] Ibid., 11.
[140] http://en.wikipedia.org/wiki/Reincarnation

Chapter Seventeen

[141] Virginia Hummel. Miracle Messenger, (StarChild10 Publications, 2011),187-203.

Conclusion

[142] http://www.amazon.com/The-Teachings-Don-Juan-Knowledge/dp/0671600419/ref=sr_1_1?ie=UTF8&qid=1398194266&sr=8-1&keywords=The+Teachings+of+Don+Juan%2C

About the Author

Virginia M. Hummel, is a writer, speaker, and co-producer of an upcoming documentary on healing grief through Spiritually Transformative Experiences (STEs). Her deepest hope is to help guide others on a spiritual path to transmute pain, loss and grief into personal growth and empowerment.

She is a lifelong student of metaphysical, spiritual and after-death subjects. With the death of her youngest son, Christopher, she experienced a series of spontaneous spiritual events that helped transform her grief and find a place of balance and joy.

Virginia has been a researcher and experiencer of the orb phenomenon for over a decade and is Chairman of Orb Encounters at **Eternea.org**, a publicly supported global non-profit research, educational and outreach organization co-created by Eben Alexander and John Audette. Eternea's mission is to advance research, education and applied programs concerning the physics of consciousness and the interactive relationship between consciousness and physical reality.

Please visit her at: **Virginiahummel.com** dedicated to healing grief through Spiritually Transformative Experiences (STEs), and **OrbWhisperer.com** dedicated to the orb phenomenon.

Also by Virginia Hummel

Orbs and the Afterlife:
Survival of the Soul

Miracle Messenger:
Signs from Above, Love from Beyond

Dying To Fit In
Erica McKenzie with Virginia M. Hummel
Foreword by Dr. Rajiv Parti

Available at Amazon.com
Paperback
Kindle

Made in the USA
Las Vegas, NV
15 November 2021